CW00661427

A Christ...
an Unbe...
Discuss...

Life, the Universe and Everything

LifeStyles

yOne

Rob Slane

Endorsements for *The God Reality*

A most effective response to Dawkins by one who once embraced and used atheistic arguments, but who now refutes them in a way which will secure the respect of all readers.

The Metropolitan Tabernacle Book Catalogue

Rob Slane takes several of Dawkins' leading arguments, calmly examines them, shows the illogicality of them and provides a biblical answer. The author himself was an atheist before his conversion and so writes with understanding and passion. We strongly recommend this book for anyone concerned with these issues.

Free Church Witness

In this little book, Rob Slane provides a succinct, helpful survey of the many imprecisions and contradictions that proliferate in the muddled mind of an atheist. By a strange twist of irony, Rob has turned Dawkins' God Delusion into a wonderful apologetic for the Christian faith!

Kevin Swanson, Host, Generations Radio, Director, Generations with Vision, and Pastor of Reformation Church OPC, Colorado, USA

It should be read by all believers who desire to strengthen their faith with reason, but also agnostics who are really seeking the truth. They will find a lot of important arguments in it.

Prof. Dr hab Wojciech Roszkowski, Institute of Political Studies of the Polish Academy of Sciences

We warmly commend this book and urge our readers to obtain copies to give away to any who are influenced by Dawkins' views.

The Bible League Quarterly

The God Reality *is a book which shows in full the weakness of the arguments of Richard Dawkins in* The God Delusion. *The eclectic and weak scientific apparatus used in Dawkins' narration is exposed in* The God Reality, *and should be warning to the fans of pseudo-science.*

Prof. Andrzej Kochanski, geneticist

Slane unapologetically deals with the Darwinian atheistic faith of Dawkins, which is blind to the arguments that come from geological experiments or the basis of reasoning.

Prof. Dr hab (Engineer) Adam Cenian, Institute of Fluid-Flow Machinery, Polish Academy of Sciences

What Slane does well is to expose the true weakness of the atheists' position, which is the consequence of his beliefs. The atheist has no logical basis for morality and Slane very perceptively reveals the logical (and somewhat frightening) conclusions of where Dawkins' beliefs are headed.

Evangelicals Now

There are some very helpful arguments that will help Christians who feel they ought to read Dawkins' book.

Evangelical Times

© Day One Publications 2015

ISBN 978-1-84625-448-2

Unless otherwise indicated, all Scripture quotations are from the King James (Authorized) Version (KJV), Crown copyright, and from The Holy Bible, English Standard Version, published by HarperCollinsPublishers © 2001 by Crossway Bibles, a division of Good News Publishers. Used by permission. All rights reserved.

British Library Cataloguing in Publication Data available

Published by Day One Publications
Ryelands Road, Leominster, HR6 8NZ
Telephone 01568 613 740 FAX 01568 611 473
email—sales@dayone.co.uk
web site—www.dayone.co.uk

All rights reserved
No part of this publication may be reproduced, or stored in a retrieval system, or transmitted, in any form or by any means, mechanical, electronic, photocopying, recording or otherwise, without the prior permission of Day One Publications.

Cover design by Rob Jones, Elk Design
Printed by TJ International

Dedication
To George, Marta, Joseph,
Samuel, Rachel and Benjamin:
my six amazing, smart, funny,
eccentric, dippy and delightful
children

Acknowledgements

I would like to thank my good friends Alan Finch and Benjamin Merkle for looking at this work and making various helpful comments and suggestions. I would also like to thank Jim Holmes and Mark Roberts at Day One for agreeing to take on what is a bit of an odd book, along with Caroline McCausland and Suzanne Mitchell for getting the text ready for publishing. And of course, I would like to thank Alina, the best wife imaginable, for all her comments and for her graciousness in putting up with my not talking to her during the long hours in which this book was written.

Contents

PREFACE   8

A JOURNEY BEGINS   10

OBJECTION 1:   OKAY, IF GOD EXISTS, PROVE IT   13

OBJECTION 2:   SCIENCE HAS DISPROVED GOD   23

OBJECTION 3:   IF GOD IS SO GOOD, WHY DOES HE ALLOW EVIL?   34

OBJECTION 4:   YOU DON'T NEED TO BELIEVE IN GOD TO BE MORAL   48

OBJECTION 5:   WHAT IS TRUTH?   58

OBJECTION 6:   CHRISTIANITY IS IRRATIONAL   69

OBJECTION 7:   RELIGION IS JUST A CRUTCH FOR PEOPLE WHO CAN'T FACE REALITY   81

OBJECTION 8:   NOBODY BELIEVES THE BIBLE ANY MORE   93

OBJECTION 9:   CHRISTIANITY HAS FAILED TO FULFIL ITS PROMISES   104

OBJECTION 10: GIVE ME ONE GOOD REASON WHY I SHOULD BELIEVE WHAT YOU BELIEVE   116

JOURNEY'S END   125

Preface

It may seem a little odd for an apologetics book to begin with an apologetic about the book, but in this case I think it may well be necessary and wise. I know that nobody really reads prefaces, so I have kept this deliberately short in the hope that you might stop by before going on to main part of the book.

The book you hold in your hands exposes many of the divisions between Christians and unbelievers, yet it may well have the remarkable ability to unite both camps on one point. It is quite possible that it could have the effect of infuriating both Christians and unbelievers alike, and pleasing nobody in particular. The book contains a conversation between two men who meet on a train, and I anticipate that readers from both camps could equally well find themselves saying things like, 'I wouldn't have put it like that,' or 'He should have said such and such.'

However, before you find yourself becoming exasperated at the stubbornness of the Christian or the obtuseness of the unbeliever, or vice versa, I would point out that the conversation is meant to be just that: a conversation. It is in no way intended to be an academic treatment of the subjects discussed, and it is in no way intended to cover every angle of the subjects discussed; rather it is intended to be the sort of conversation that could realistically occur between two ordinary people on a train over an hour and a half.

Of the two camps, though, I anticipate that those on the unbelieving side may well be the most disgruntled, since I, the author, am on the side of the Christian and therefore am keen to see his arguments do well. In my defence, I should mention that all of the arguments put forward by the unbeliever are either points that I have come across as a Christian in discussions with unbelievers, or ones that I used myself when I was an unbeliever. Nothing of the general substance of the discussion has been made up.

So if you find yourself tearing your hair out because one character or other responded in the 'wrong way', or missed the opportunity to mention such and such, I agree wholeheartedly. He probably did. But then that's the nature of all such discussions: you always find yourself analysing afterwards whether you should have said this, or shouldn't have said that, or if you could have said something better. And the answer to all three concerns is probably 'yes'. But don't let that put you off.

Rob Slane

A journey begins

It was on a chilly day in mid-October that I made my way into the concourse at Waterloo Station to catch my train home. I had no idea what time the train was due to leave, and the main electronic display screens appeared to be about as much use as the proverbial chocolate kettle. So I strolled over to the ticket office and had a look at the timetables. When I found my destination and saw what time the train was due to leave, I glanced at my watch and saw that I had less than three minutes to go. The next train was due in an hour. Anyone familiar with Waterloo Station will know that running from the ticket office to a train in little over two minutes would be easily achievable were it not for the fact that there are usually several hundred people between you and your train.

So I treated several amused onlookers to a performance of the 'dance of the undecided commuter'. You know, when you look at your watch, measure the distance in your mind, look at the number of people in between you and the platforms, decide you might just be able to make it, begin to set off, stop because it dawns on you that it is a hopeless business and not worth getting all out of breath for, suddenly remember that if you don't make it you've got another hour to wait, castigate yourself for having wasted ten seconds um-ing and ah-ing, set off, then stop and repeat the whole business again, all the while appearing faintly ridiculous, before setting off for the final time, playing 'dodge the commuters' at an even faster pace than you would have done had you not stopped in the first place.

I had a rough idea which platform my train would be leaving from, so I was able to quickly establish which one I needed to enter. Nevertheless, I still had one or two of those pangs of paranoia that you get when you realize that you haven't had nearly enough time to make absolutely sure that it is really the correct platform and you suddenly suspect that you will shortly find yourself travelling in a direction not wholly conducive to getting you to your home. But as providence had it, I had indeed got the correct platform, and I made it on to my train with little more than ten seconds to spare—a very happy man, I might add.

Panting for breath, and realizing that I might have lost a wee bit of fitness in recent years, I walked down the aisle of the carriage to get a seat. The train was fairly empty, and although normally I would have sat down on a double seat, I headed straight for one of the four-seaters—two double seats facing each other with a table in between. As I put my bag down, I noticed that there was a man sitting in the opposite seat and that he was wearing a faintly amused expression on his face as he saw me panting and wheezing as if I was ready to drop. I grinned back at him and said something about running for trains being an integral part of the new fitness regime I had adopted.

As the train began to pull out of the station, I opened my bag and put the following contents on the table in front of me: a ham sandwich, a banana, a bottle of water, a copy of the first part of *The Lord of the Rings* and my Bible. I then placed the bag in the overhead luggage rack and sat down to catch my breath.

I spent a minute or so looking out of the window at Waterloo disappearing behind us before turning back towards the guy opposite me. I noticed that his expression had changed from one of amusement to more of a frown. I also noticed that—somewhat curiously—he also had a ham sandwich, a banana, a bottle of water and—would you believe it—a copy of *The Lord of the Rings*, albeit the second part in the trilogy. I thought perhaps that his change of expression had something to do with being a little freaked out by this bizarre coincidence, but on closer inspection I saw that this was not the reason at all. For I now noticed that he had not only a copy of *The Lord of the Rings* with him, but also Richard Dawkins' *The God Delusion*. I supposed that he could have been reading it merely out of curiosity, but something in the way that he was looking at me and my Bible suggested otherwise.

'Mmm,' I thought, 'could be interesting.' But in the end, it was he who broke the ice:

'I suppose you're going to start evangelizing me.'

Pretty forward, I thought. But never mind, should make for a more interesting train journey than normal.

'Funny,' I replied with a smile, 'I was just about to say the same thing to you.'

He looked at me attentively for a few seconds, as if he were weighing up whether he should or shouldn't bother pursuing the matter. I toyed with the idea of trying to lighten the atmosphere by offering to fling his copy of *The God Delusion* out of the window on the grounds that he already had a copy of *The Lord of the Rings* with him and surely one work of fantasy ought to suffice. But before the words formed in my mouth, he continued tongue-in-cheek:

'You know, I used to believe in Santa Claus when I was a child. But then I grew out of it.'

Like I said—not exactly backward in coming forward. Of course, what he said is nothing more than a fashionable, if rather cheap, trick linking belief in God with belief in all sorts of childish fantasies. It is probably best dealt with in like manner, so I replied:

'That's interesting. You see, I never did believe in Santa as a child, nor in God, for that matter. In fact, I only came to believe in God as an adult, after looking at the irrationality of the other "explanations" for Life, the Universe and Everything. Whereas you, on the other hand, tell me that you did believe in Santa as a child. And I'm just wondering—is it possible that there may be some connection between your childish belief in Santa and the fact that you presumably now believe that you are an evolved monkey living in a chance universe?'

Without answering my point, he folded his arms, sat back in his chair as if he were in this for the long haul and thrust forth his opening gambit.

'Okay,' he said. 'If God exists, prove it.'

Objection 1: Okay, if God exists, prove it

I had just about managed to get my breath back by this time and was now able to think straight. I looked at this chap in front of me and pondered the conversation that was about to ensue. He looked to be about the same age as me, and as already noted he appeared to share the same taste in sandwiches, fruit and novels. No doubt there were countless other similarities between us, and yet with his copy of *The God Delusion* and with my copy of the Bible, something seemed to suggest that we were poles apart on the most fundamental question a man can ever ask himself: Does God really exist?

Before I began to answer his question, I said a silent prayer, asking God to help me answer this man's questions as best as I could. Then I began:

'Okay, before I answer your question, I have a question or two for you. Tell me: What if I can't prove the existence of God? Will my not being able to prove it prove that he doesn't exist, and will you sit there and say, "There, I told you so—there is no God"? Or will it simply prove that I am unable to prove the existence of God?'

'I take it from that that you can't prove it then,' he replied, ignoring my question and with a good dose of sarcasm in his voice.

'But what if I can prove the existence of God?' I carried on, ignoring his comment. 'What will you do then? Will you get down on your knees, repent of all your sins and beg for his forgiveness? And will you then strive to keep his commandments out of love for him?'

This didn't move him one bit, and he simply repeated his original challenge. I decided I would begin by turning the tables on him by asking him if he could prove to me the non-existence of God, knowing full well what sort of response this would bring.

'The onus is not on me to prove that he doesn't exist,' replied the atheist. 'You are the one making a positive proposition about the existence of something that I can't see, and so the onus is on you to back it up with proof. I, on the other hand, am not making a positive proposition at all. I am simply denying the authenticity of yours until you give me sufficient proof that it is true. But you can't, because there is not a shred of evidence anywhere that this God,' he said, pointing at my Bible, 'actually exists.'

Well, it seemed to me from our short conversation so far that he had pretty well reached a final decision that there is no God. And so it struck me as being a trifle ungenerous of him to ask me for evidence when he had already concluded that no evidence could possibly exist, wouldn't you say?

It's rather like being cross-examined by a particularly overzealous police officer who asks you to prove your whereabouts on such and such a day, but when you give him a dozen bits of evidence that you were in a certain place at a certain time, he simply waves his hands dismissively and says, 'You weren't there. I know you weren't there. You cannot have been there. There is no evidence that you were there, and it's impossible for you to provide me with any evidence that you were there because you weren't there, and so no evidence could ever exist to show that you were there. Now, prove to me that you were there.' Not really what you'd call open to reason, if you catch my drift.

I toyed with the idea of calling it a day there and then. But something about this man's manner suggested to me that, although he clearly wasn't what you would call a seeker, he wasn't necessarily an out-and-out scorner, and it might be worth pursuing the matter a little further. So instead of quitting there and then, I laid my cards on the table:

'Okay,' I said, holding my hands up to admit my 'guilt'. 'I admit it. I am unable to prove the existence of God. I have faith. So my position is hopelessly irrational, right?'

'Right you are,' he said.

'Then I hope you won't think I'm being facetious, but aren't you in exactly the same condition? Whether you think the onus is on me to prove my case is neither here nor there. You know that you can't prove your claim that there is no God any more than I can prove my claim that there is a God, which seems to suggest that you are as reliant on "faith" as I am. And since faith is apparently hopelessly irrational, it would seem that I am not the only hopeless irrationalist in this carriage today!'

'Nice try,' he replied, 'but it won't do to judge me as irrational, because I am not trying to prove anything in the first place. You are the one coming up with the positive assertion that you can't prove. As I said before, there is no obligation on me to disprove your irrational assertion, and the fact that I can't is no reflection on my position. Did you ever hear of Russell's Teapot?'

'Russell's Teapot?' I repeated. 'You mean Bertrand Russell, the great sceptic? Yes, I do remember reading about it once. Apparently Russell was so utterly inept at doing anything practical at all, that when his wife left him in the house—the third of four wives, in the midst of his many mistresses and other brief adulteries, by the way—she used to leave him little notes with instructions on how to do the most menial of tasks. One of them had to do with making tea and, if my memory serves me correctly, said: "Move kettle onto hotplate. Wait for it to boil. Pour water from kettle into teapot." But sadly he still apparently failed to make the tea.[1] Was this what you meant by Russell's Teapot?'

He looked disdainfully at me before reaching into his pocket and fishing out his mobile phone. After a minute or so of tap-tap-tapping, he looked up and exclaimed, 'Aha! Listen, this is what Bertrand Russell said:

Many orthodox people speak as though it were the business of sceptics to disprove received dogmas rather than of dogmatists to prove them. This is, of course, a mistake. If I were to suggest that between the Earth and Mars there is a china teapot revolving about the sun in an elliptical orbit, nobody would be able to disprove my assertion provided I were careful to add that the teapot is too small to be revealed even by our most powerful telescopes. But if I were to go on to say that, since my assertion cannot be disproved, it is intolerable presumption on the part of human reason to doubt it, I should rightly be thought to be talking nonsense. If, however, the existence of such a teapot were affirmed in ancient books, taught as the sacred truth every Sunday, and instilled into the minds of children at school, hesitation to believe in its existence would become a mark of eccentricity and entitle the doubter to the attentions of the psychiatrist in an enlightened age or of the Inquisitor in an earlier time.[2]

After he had finished reading the passage, he turned the phone off, laid it on the table and said, 'What do you say to that, then?'

'I believe that Mr Russell esteemed himself quite a moral philosopher,' I replied. 'He seemed to think he had a good deal of the answers to the problems facing the world. Only problem was, he wasn't even able to sort out his own life and his own problems. Did I mention his three divorces?'

'What's that got to do with it?' replied the atheist.

'Rather a lot, I would have thought,' I replied. 'If someone is going to set themselves up as a moral guru with the answers for the salvation of humanity, I would think that a good place to see whether there is anything in their message would be to look at what that person is like around their family and friends. I doubt very much that anyone with Russell's ability to change wives when he got fed up with them, or they with him, is really going to have the solution to the problems facing a lost and lonely world. Very easy to write theoretical solutions to all the world's ills; much more difficult to do those practical things that would actually make some difference. It reminds me of the words of P. J. O'Rourke: "Everybody wants to save the earth; nobody wants to help mum do the dishes."'[3]

'Well, whatever,' said the atheist. 'You still haven't answered his Teapot.'

'Ah yes, the Teapot,' I said. 'Well, I admit that at first glance it does seem pretty plausible. I suppose that if anyone did propose that there is a china teapot revolving around the sun between Earth and Mars, the onus—if anybody else actually cared—would indeed be on them to prove it.'

'Exactly!' cried the atheist in a somewhat triumphant voice.

'But I think that Bertie was being a little disingenuous in comparing this with God,' I went on. 'For a start, in his illustration, the man proposing the revolving teapot is proposing something quite new and quite novel, and so it is indeed up to him to prove his claim. Not so with God. Do you know of any society in history where the numbers of people believing in some sort of higher being were in the minority? Now, don't get me wrong. I'm not using the "majority must be right" argument to try and prove the point. That's dangerous territory. All I'm saying is that before Mr Teapot came along, nobody had ever proposed this, and so the onus was clearly on him to prove his claim.

'But in the case of God, it is Bertrand Russell, and indeed you, my friend, who are more truly in the position of Mr Teapot. Throughout history, men everywhere have had some sort of belief in the divine, which kind of suggests that there may just be some truth in it. And no, they weren't all indoctrinated into it in Sunday school or from ancient books as Russell suggested. They simply believed it because it appeared obvious to them that life doesn't tend to spring up all by itself. But now along come the New Atheists, and without actually producing a shred more evidence than the ancients had that life sprang up all by itself, they propose that life did indeed spring up all by itself. So I'm afraid I beg to differ with Bertie on this one. It appears to me that the onus ought to be on the man who dismisses the entire testimony of human history to show us what he has discovered to disprove it all.

'Secondly,' I continued, 'it's interesting that when Russell wrote these words, it was indeed true that the majority of children in Western countries were brought up in their homes, schools and Sunday schools with the existence of God "instilled into their minds", as he says. But now look at things. The exact opposite is true, and the majority of children are now brought up in homes and schools where there is virtually no mention of God, which is as good as denying the existence of God. Instead, they are indoctrinated into evolutionism, which is drummed into them by their schools, the media and often their parents. Hesitating to believe these apparent "truths" is now the mark of eccentricity, and it is those who doubt these "truths" rather than those who accept them who are more likely to be subject to the attentions of the psychiatrist.

'But the biggest flaw in his argument,' I went on, 'is in comparing a miniscule teapot, which could never leave any stamp of its existence on the universe or on anyone's life, with God, who could never fail to leave a stamp of his existence on the universe or on everyone's life. Mr Teapot is on a hiding to nothing. He can produce no evidence for the teapot's existence, because other than itself, the teapot can produce no evidence for its existence. But for believers in the Creator of the universe, we can produce an abundance of evidence for his existence because he has produced an abundance of evidence.'

'Okay, like what?' he said, as he took a bite of his ham sandwich.

'You're eating some of it right now,' I replied immediately.

'You what?' he said, nearly choking.

'That's right,' I continued. 'Even your ham sandwich is evidence. If God exists, then all things have been created by him. Therefore, literally everything is evidence for his existence, regardless of whether you choose to accept it or not. From aardvarks through ham sandwiches, all the way up to zygotes, everything is evidence.'

'Sorry to disappoint you,' he replied, mumbling as he polished off the remains of his mouthful, 'but that's just circular reasoning: "If God exists then everything in the universe is evidence of God's existence. Ergo, the fact that everything in the universe exists proves the existence of God." You'll have to do a lot better than that, I'm afraid.'

'You're right,' I replied, smiling at him, 'but unfortunately for you, your position belongs in exactly the same category of circular reasoning: "There is no God, and all things have come into existence without God. Ergo, the fact that all things exist and didn't need God to create them proves the non-existence of God." Which is why the question of providing evidence is such a disingenuous one in the first place. I look at a frog, for example, and I say that this frog is evidence of a Creator God. You look at a frog and say that this is a product of evolution and therefore evidence that there is no Creator God. So the question "What proof or evidence can you give me?" is really rather futile. A more interesting and pertinent question is "Which explanation—God or Godless—best fits the evidence we have in the world we live in?"'

He beckoned me to continue, so I gave him a few examples of what I was hinting at.

Take the soul and emotions, for example. Go ahead and explain this through the eyes of unbelief. If you begin with God, it's incredibly simple. God created man in his own image, which meant, among other things, giving him a reasonable soul with the capacity for emotions. And that's it. But any atheist's explanation, on the other hand, is bound to be far more complex, far more convoluted and ultimately ham-fisted, partly because it must explain how it was that for (allegedly) billions of years the soul and emotions were non-existent on planet Earth but then somehow—almost miraculously, you might say—these things suddenly came into existence. Or you might want to look at morality. If you begin with God, again this is easy. God imprinted his moral character on man in the act of creating him. That's all there is to it.

But try explaining it from the atheistic position. If you are going to go down the road of using evolution and natural selection to explain this phenomenon, you will find yourself getting into all sorts of knots. For example, can survival of the fittest—which is amoral by its very nature— really explain how all humans have some concept of right and wrong? Moreover, can it explain why it is that our morality often disapproves of actions that are perfectly in tune with the Darwinian notion of survival of the fittest? Many other things could be mentioned that you will be hard pushed to explain through atheism but which are explained neatly and simply in the first few chapters of the Bible: the universality of the seven-day week throughout the globe; why man has invented a whole host of different religions; the institution of marriage; why we have to work by the sweat of our brow but the supposedly 'less evolved animals' do not; the origin of languages, and so on. Atheists must produce reams and reams of stuff trying—and ultimately failing—to provide satisfactory explanations for these things, whereas the Bible's explanation is not only simpler but in complete accordance with the facts it purports to explain, tying in perfectly with what we find in ourselves, in each other and in society at large. It is just as Romans 1:19 says: 'That which may be known of God is manifest in them; for God hath shewed it unto them.'

When I quoted this verse, the atheist tossed his head back in disgust and said disdainfully, 'Oh please, you're not going to start quoting Scripture at me, are you?'

'Well, what do you expect me to do?' I replied. 'If you're going to attack the Bible—which is what you are doing—then how do you expect me to defend it without quoting it? If we were discussing *The Lord of the Rings* and I claimed that Frodo Baggins dies when the Ring is cast into the fire of Mount Doom, would you not pick up a copy of the book and read to me the bit when the Ring is cast into the fire of Mount Doom, just to refute the claim I had made? And would it not be rather churlish of me to disallow you the right to do so?'

'Okay,' he said, 'point taken. But getting back to the real issue, you've given me loads of so-called evidence, but you still haven't given me a shred of proof for your claim.'

'You're right,' I said. 'I haven't given you any proof. But the problem is that I'm a little unsure what you mean by proof. You see, I have mentioned a few things that I had supposed were perfectly good pieces of evidence— biblical explanations that fit in with reality—but none of these have satisfied you. Perhaps if you could define to me what you mean by "proof" then we might get somewhere.'

It was fairly clear from the way he hesitated after my request that, although he had used the 'proof' objection many times before, he had never actually thought about what he meant by it and so had no answer. As he was pondering how to respond, I continued:

'Could it be that your trouble is not lack of evidence, but rather your insistence on absolute proof, which is an entirely irrational demand to make? Let me tell you a little story to illustrate the point. There was once a trial in which a man was accused of shooting his wife. Although the man pleaded not guilty, every piece of evidence heard in the courtroom pointed to the accused man having carried out the crime: he had suspected his wife of committing adultery, and so he had a motive; her blood was found on his clothing; he had bought a gun the day before the murder, and forensics had shown with 99 per cent certainty that this was the gun that was used to kill the woman; and two witnesses had seen him that night struggling to put a very large sack into the boot of his car, which was later found to contain traces of his wife's blood. But in the jury room after the trial, only eleven jurors found the man guilty, while one of them returned a not-guilty verdict. When the eleven asked the one for his reasons, do you know what he said?'

The atheist shook his head.

'He said this: "Really, I'm afraid I cannot tell one way or another whether the man is guilty. I know they said he had a motive, but then again perhaps there are others who had a similar motive—how am I to know? I know it was said that her blood was found on his clothing, but I cannot rule out the possibility that this was planted there. I know that the forensic experts are 99 per cent certain that the gun he bought was the murder weapon, but the 1 per cent uncertainty makes me more than a little queasy, and in any case, whether or not he bought the gun provides no proof whatsoever that he actually used it. As for the witnesses, I heard all they said, but how am I to know if they are telling the truth or not? All in all, we have been given no absolute proof whatsoever that this man was the murderer." Now tell me, do you think that this man was acting in a rational manner?'

'No, of course not,' said the atheist.

'Well, in one sense he was,' I replied. 'He was correct in saying that neither he nor his fellow jurors had been given proof in the absolute sense of the word. But since the only way that they could have had such absolute proof would have been if they had personally seen the man murdering his wife, in another sense he was acting entirely irrationally. In other words, by trying to follow the path of rationality to the letter, in seeking absolute proof in order to convict a man, he ended up discarding all the perfectly good evidence that clearly pointed to the guilt of the accused. He didn't understand that his desire for absolute proof was a foolish one, because it could never be satisfied, unless he had personally seen the man committing the murder, and even then he might have explained it away as a dream or an illusion or a delusion. All that was required of him was that he examine the evidence presented to him and come to a decision based on the balance of reasonable probabilities. The point I am making is that if you approach the question of God's existence in the same manner as the man in the courtroom, you will end up rejecting the mass of perfectly good evidence which all points towards his existence. So let me ask you once more: When you demand that I prove the existence of God to you, what exactly is this proof that you are demanding?'

'What I am demanding,' he replied, 'is that you give me something that can be empirically proven. Simply saying that God made aardvarks or ham sandwiches or frogs or whatever is in no way empirical, and it is in no way scientific.'

'Ah, science,' I groaned, 'the great god that rules the age.'

'Ah! I might have known you'd be opposed to science,' he groaned in response. 'Well, that's just too bad, because I'm afraid here your "faith" dies the death. Didn't you know? Science has disproved God.'

Notes

1 Quoted in Paul Johnson, *Intellectuals* (London: Weidenfeld & Nicolson, 1988), p. 202.
2 Quoted in Richard Dawkins, *The God Delusion* (London: Black Swan, 2007), pp. 74–75.
3 P. J. O'Rourke, *All the Trouble in the World* (New York: Atlantic Monthly Press, 1994), p. 9.

Objection 2: Science has disproved God

D ue to the chilly weather outside, the heaters in the train were going full blast, and it was now so warm that I had to take my coat and jumper off. As I laid them on the seat next to me, I decided that if the conversation was to continue for a while, which looked fairly likely, I ought to introduce myself and also find out a bit about him. He told me that his name was Alex and that he was married and had a couple of children. He worked for an insurance firm, and he travelled down to London once a month to the company's head office.

For a few moments we broke off our conversation about Life, the Universe and Everything and spent a few minutes discussing *The Lord of the Rings*, followed by what our wives were making for dinner that night and then the many and varied difficulties of trying to get our children to sit at the dining table without wobbling on their chairs to the point that they almost, but not quite, toppled over. Our conclusions? The curious thing with *The Lord of the Rings* is that it always looks far too long when you start reading and seems much too short when you've finished; probably sausages; and that no matter what measures we took to stop our children from wobbling on their chairs to the point that they almost, but not quite, toppled over, they would probably only learn at the point when they wobbled just that little bit too far and finally fell off. And even if this happened, it was still by no means certain that they would not do it again.

But by and by, the conversation tailed off naturally, and we soon returned to our former discussion.

'Can I borrow this for a moment?' I asked, pointing to his mobile, which he had used to look up Russell's Teapot. He nodded, and after a few moments of searching, I found what I was looking for.

'Here's a dictionary definition of the word "science": "The systematic study of the nature and behaviour of the material and physical universe, based on observation and measurement by experimentation."[1] Are you happy with that definition?'

'Yes, I suppose so,' he replied.

'Well then, if you are claiming that science has proved the non-existence of God, or at the very least done away with the need for God, then I'm afraid you are going to have to do one of two things: either you're going to have to redefine God to have him belong to the material and physical universe so that he can be observed and measured by experimentation, or you're going to have to redefine the word "science" so that it includes the study of the nature and behaviour of the non-material and non-physical universe. But since God clearly isn't of the same essence as the material and physical universe—if he did he wouldn't be God—and since science cannot observe and study the non-material and non-physical universe, I'd say that there might just be a slight problem in stating that science has or even can disprove the existence of God, don't you think?'

'Not at all,' he replied. 'All I have to do is show how science can explain the universe without invoking the non-material and non-physical.'

'Okay,' I said, 'in that case, can you tell me of all the observations and experiments you know of that have done this?'

He replied by telling me how the Big Bang provides a totally adequate explanation for the universe and how evolution is a more than adequate explanation for life as we know it. For good measure, he added that by far the majority of the world's scientists accept these explanations, which seemed to imply that I, along with any other such troublemakers, should therefore pipe down and accept their verdict with good grace as if it were written on tablets of stone. I'm not quite sure why anyone should think that we ought to attach any importance to the fact that there are more scientists who choose to believe these explanations than the biblical explanation, and I couldn't resist pointing out to Alex how ironic it is that many unbelievers will go on about the brainwashing effects of 'religion' while accepting unquestioningly what the 'gods' in the lab coats say.

But even leaving aside the question of what scientists have to say about God, I pointed out to Alex that he hadn't actually answered my question at all. What I had asked him for was observations and experiments that proved the non-existence of God. With the best will in the world, neither the Big Bang nor the origins of life are verifiable by observation or by experimentation.

'As for the credibility of these explanations,' I said, 'have you ever sat down and thought about what it is all these scientists are really saying behind all the technical jargon that they use to make their claims seem credible?'

'Go on,' he said.

'Well, let's take the origins of the universe itself. If you fish out all the complicated "scientific words" from the various explanations, you find that there are really only three competing theories for the existence of the universe. The first is that it came from literally nothing—that is, no matter, no time, no space and no energy. The second is that it came from pre-existing matter and energy. And the third is that it was created by an eternal, personal being whose essence is other than the universe he created.'

'And I suppose you're going to tell me that only the third is plausible,' he said.

'No, I'm going to point out the logical fallacies of the first two and let you make your own mind up,' I said, tongue firmly in cheek. 'As for the first theoretical possibility, the central problem with this position is not difficult to pinpoint. Asserting that something came from nothing—and I mean by that absolutely nothing, no time, no space, no matter and no energy—does tend to run contrary to all experience and logic. Those who hold to this so-called scientific position are thus taking a massive "leap of faith" in the dark.

'As for the second group, they have two problems that they can't answer. Firstly, matter does not create new matter, and secondly, however plausibly they might like to dress up their claims for the origins of our time-space-matter-energy universe, the one thing their theory utterly fails to explain is the origins of time, space, matter and energy, because it assumes their prior existence. Theirs is perhaps not quite as great a "leap of faith" as the first group's, but it is still a desperate and self-refuting attempt to explain what exists without having to bring in God.'

'And on that subject,' he interjected, 'you speak about a leap of faith, but the greatest leap of faith of all is the idea that because we can't quite get our heads around how the universe came from nothing or from pre-existing matter, we must resort to God—the last refuge of the desperate—to explain it all. One small problem with this, though: God fails on the same point as the other two explanations. If something cannot come from nothing, but needs something else to produce it, then this must apply to God. On the other hand, if nothing can exist eternally, then the idea of the eternal God is sheer folly. It's the old "If God made the universe, who made God?" problem which you cannot answer.'

It sounds plausible on the surface, doesn't it? But the error in this way of thinking is that it confuses that which humans do know with that which we don't know. We have enough knowledge to be able to assert that 'pure nothingness' cannot produce 'something'. We also have enough knowledge to be able to assert that matter does not create matter, nor can it be eternally existing. But do we have enough knowledge to assert that a being whose essence is spirit cannot create matter? And do we have enough knowledge to assert that a non-material spirit cannot be eternally existing?

The simple truth is that, in and of ourselves, we don't. Our knowledge and experience are entirely confined to the time-space-matter universe to which we belong, and they do not extend to an eternally existing spirit. Which is why the 'If God made the universe, who made God?' question is so disingenuous. The question is just man looking around at the universe he exists in and seeing that it cannot possibly have created itself or been eternally existent. Then instead of concluding—as logic would suggest— that it must have been created by something outside the material universe, he actually uses his observation to proclaim that it cannot have been created by a something outside the material universe. And then he goes back to believing in one or other of the two falsehoods that he wrongly used to proclaim the death of God!

It's a bit like a man looking at the Great Pyramid of Giza, scratching his beard and shaking his head in bemusement, saying, 'Now just how on earth did they get those stones there without using lorries and giant excavators?' Although he can't fathom this out, he does at least know two things: firstly, that the stones did not just appear there from nothing, and secondly, that they did not get there by themselves. But the more he tries to understand how the men of those days could have put these stones into position, the more he fails to understand it—so much so that in the end he dismisses the idea, shrugs his shoulders and says, 'Oh well, I suppose they must have appeared there or got there by themselves after all.' Such thinking may be many things, but logical, rational and reasonable it certainly isn't!

'But let's just suppose for a moment that either of the "non-God" explanations were plausible,' I continued. 'What good would that do you?'

'What do you mean?' he replied.

'Well, if I can explain the universe by invoking the omnipotent God, I'm not going to have a great deal of trouble explaining anything that follows. The probability of such a God being capable of making a universe is exactly one. The probability of such a God being capable of creating life is exactly one. But with either of the two "non-God" explanations, you still have the problem of explaining how the first life form actually came into being.

'I remember reading Dawkins' explanation of this in *The God Delusion*. It was tucked away in one of those sentences that gives the impression he would rather not have had to put it in but knew he had to or some little boy somewhere out there might have blurted out, "Hey, everyone, look! Dawkins has got no clothes on!" And do you know what he said? He said that life needed "some luck to get it started".[2] What was that? Sorry, I didn't quite catch that, Richard, old boy. Did you say it needed some luck? You mean the mechanism whereby dust suddenly became a living creature was some luck? Well, isn't that just grand!

Doesn't that make all the sense in the world! Isn't that science at its very best! And doesn't it make you glad that we've got such great scientific minds around who can give us the answers to all these difficult questions!'

'You obviously don't have a lot of time for science and scientists,' said Alex, to which I replied that this was not the case at all; I have no problem whatsoever with embracing proper, empirical science, but resting the creation of the universe and all life forms on something called 'luck' was not science but its opposite—superstition.

We then spent the next few minutes discussing evolution itself. Like many people, Alex couldn't even contemplate the idea that evolution is not a proven fact, having seen all those wonderfully imaginative drawings of apemen in school textbooks and having had it rammed down his throat incessantly by the media. He clearly felt that anyone who questioned it must automatically believe that the earth is flat, the moon is made of cheese and that there is a tiny china teapot orbiting the sun somewhere between Earth and Mars.

But like many such people, it was pretty clear when I questioned him that he had no idea that there are two very different types of evolution: microevolution, which takes place within kinds and which all creationists agree is a fact because it can be observed in front of their own eyes, and macroevolution, which allegedly takes place from one kind to another and which is not a fact because no examples—fossil or living—exist to back it up. Of course, Alex disputed this and said that there was plenty of evidence in the fossil record to prove it.

So I asked him what he thought I should expect the fossil record to look like if it is indeed a monument of our evolutionary past. For instance, how long would it take a fish to turn into an amphibian? A hundred years? He said that it would presumably take millions. Why is that? I asked him. Because it would need such great spans of time for the gradual changes to take place over many, many generations. And over a period of, say, 100 million years, a species of fish turning into a species of amphibian might need how many minute changes? A hundred? He said that it would presumably require tens, if not hundreds, of thousands.

And how many fish might make this transition? A hundred? He said that he supposed there would be millions of fish. In which case, I asked (keeping the number deliberately conservative, as clearly not all fish would necessarily be fossilized), am I being reasonable to expect that a fossil record documenting, say, 10,000 changes in, say, a million fish ought to contain at least a million examples of semi-fish-semi-amphibians? He supposed this to be reasonable. So why is it that there is slightly less than one example? And never minding the fossil record, why is it that among all the billions of living fish today there appears to be slightly less than one example of a transitional species? Are they all in hiding? Or have they all been caught and eaten by wicked creationists trying to remove all the evidence?

Ignoring my sarcasm, Alex returned to the more general theme of science.

'What you're really saying is that science has nothing to say about the existence of God. Is that right?' he asked.

'Yes and no,' I replied.

'What's that supposed to mean?' he said, looking a little baffled.

'Well, if you ask me if I think that the existence of God is a scientific question rather than a faith question, then I would answer unequivocally that it is,' I said. 'The existence or the non-existence of God is scientific in that it is a fact one way or the other, however much people may agree or disagree on the issue down here on planet Earth. Either God exists or God doesn't exist, and nothing any of us say or think or do can alter this one iota. If he does exist, your faith in his non-existence is not going to make the slightest bit of difference to that fact. And if he doesn't exist, my faith in his existence is not going to change that one jot. Agreed?'

He nodded.

'But the mistake that the atheistic scientists and philosophers make is to suppose that this "scientific question" can be answered by using their own scientific means, which, according to the dictionary definition I read out earlier, belong purely to the material and physical world.'

'Are you telling me it can't be answered?' he replied.

'Well, that would depend entirely on whether God allows them to find him out in this way. Scientists seem to believe that if God exists, they would be able to find him out using their own wit and invention, and they assume that, because they haven't uncovered what they perceive to be incontrovertible proof of his existence, this means that he doesn't exist.'

Once again I used Alex's mobile, this time to look up the following quote from Charles Darwin: 'Despite all my powers of deluding myself, it became more and more difficult to find proof enough to satisfy me, and that is how faithlessness stalked me and took hold over me slowly, till I became totally disbelieving.'[3]

'Now let's play "spot the problem with Darwin's thinking",' I said. 'Could it be that in assuming that God would actually allow himself to be discovered by what Darwin would have called "scientific means", and that in assuming God is somehow under obligation to reveal himself using such means, Darwin was mistaken? Could he have said these words if he'd read and understood this rhetorical question in the book of Job (11:7): "Canst thou by searching find out God?"'

'Hold on a minute,' said Alex. 'Are you telling me that this God of yours, who allegedly created us and gave us all rational minds, denies us the ability to know whether he exists or not by the use of the rational minds he has created? That doesn't sound very rational!'

'No,' I replied. 'I'm not saying that he denies us the ability to find him nor that the way of finding him is irrational or unscientific—far from it. What I am saying is that it is irrational and unscientific to try to find God or prove his existence by using means that he himself disallows. You see, if God is God, and if he is as the Bible claims him to be—omnipotent and omniscient—then clearly he is able to set the rules as to how men can discover him, and he is also able to prevent them from discovering him too, if he so wishes. So by definition, the only rational and truly scientific way of discovering him would be to seek him using the means by which he says he can be discovered. On the flip side, the irrational and unscientific thing to do would be for man to try to find him out by means which God says are doomed to failure. Agreed?'

'Up to a point,' returned Alex with a slight smirk on his face. 'I suppose what you're saying is this: a man in a laboratory sets up his maze so that the rats can only find the door to the room where the man sits if they decipher the prophecies in some book written by ancient rats. If they fail to do this, they will only have themselves to blame when the man sets the maze on fire to burn them all. Agreed?'

I told Alex that I would indeed agree, provided he accepted the following criteria: that the man is perfectly benevolent towards the rats, loving them, feeding them and giving them everything that is truly good for them; that the maze is simply enormous and represents no curtailment of freedom for the rats; that the rats have been given free will but are in constant rebellion against the man, defying his laws, hating him and even denying his existence; that they all perceive themselves to be good and righteous while all the time thinking, saying and even doing much evil to one another, so much so that the man cannot have anything to do with them in this condition and on their terms; that the man continues to love the rats despite their rebellion, so much so that he is prepared to forgive them for everything if they repent; and that he gives them a perfectly legible book telling them about himself, their rebellion, his love for them and the ultimate fate that awaits them if they do not repent of their wickedness.

Unfortunately, my criteria didn't appear to be what Alex had had in mind, and he continued by saying that I still hadn't explained why it is that God, who apparently made us to glorify himself, appears to be so elusive.

'There is nothing elusive about him,' I replied. 'The Bible says those who seek him with their whole heart shall find him (Jeremiah 29:13).'

This made Alex almost jump out of his seat. 'Hold on a minute! A few moments ago you quoted a verse that implied that we can't find God by searching. And now you are quoting a verse that says that if we search for him, we shall find him. The contradiction is so obvious that I'm amazed you bother to defend your position!'

'There is no contradiction,' I replied. 'The two verses illustrate perfectly what I'm saying because they refer to two completely different ways of searching. The one mentioned in Job—"Canst thou by searching find out God?"—clearly implies man searching for God by man's methods. And it is clear from this verse that this can't be done. It is therefore unscientific to even attempt it, and utterly irrational to proclaim the non-existence of God when we can't find him using our own knowledge and wisdom. But the verse in Jeremiah refers to man searching for God using God's methods.'

'And what are those?'

'Well, they certainly have nothing to do with what humans call "science",' I replied. 'You want to know why God seems to be elusive? It is not because he doesn't want the people he created to know him—far from it. It is rather that our total rebellion against him is such a stench to him that he has been forced to withdraw himself from men. As it says in Isaiah, "Your iniquities have separated between you and your God, and your sins have hid his face from you" (Isaiah 59:2). But do you want to know how we can find this elusive God? The Bible states time and time again that the only way is to humble ourselves—"Surely he scorneth the scorners: but he giveth grace unto the lowly" (Proverbs 3:34)—and to repent of our rebellion: "The LORD is nigh unto them that are of a broken heart; and saveth such as be of a contrite spirit" (Psalm 34:18).

'That's the deal: no repentance, no revelation of God—but "seek, and ye shall find" (Matthew 7:7). So there really is no mileage whatsoever in the claim that science has disproved God—nor that it can prove him, for that matter. It can do neither. That isn't the purpose of science, and it could never do it anyway. But since God's Word clearly says that he reveals himself only to those who first acknowledge their sins and sincerely repent of them, the only truly scientific way of testing whether God really exists is to do just this: humble yourself, confess your sins and seek forgiveness. This is God's scientific experiment. But the question is, Alex, are you willing to try it?'

He pondered what I had said for a few moments and then came up with another objection—one which I had been expecting sooner or later:

'The trouble with your position,' said Alex, 'is that you're asking me to seek a God who, according to the verse you just quoted a moment or two ago, is so good that he can't have anything to do with us because of our sins. Yet it doesn't appear from the world that he actually has a great deal of problem with evil. If he did, it wouldn't exist. So answer me this: If God is so good, why does he allow evil?'

Notes

1   *Collins English Dictionary*, 6th edn. (Glasgow: HarperCollins, 2003), p. 1447.
2   Richard Dawkins, *The God Delusion* (London: Black Swan, 2007), p. 169.
3   Quoted in Christoph Marty, 'Darwin Speaks: "How Faithlessness Stalked Me"', *Scientific American*, http://www.scientificamerican.com, 11 Feb. 2009.

Objection 3: If God is so good, why does he allow evil?

In the unbeliever's eyes, this objection is checkmate, game over, thank you very much and goodbye! At this point, the believer is meant to retreat gracefully, saying, 'You know, I've never thought of that before! Well, it's been nice talking to you, and I just want to thank you for showing me the error of my ways in thinking that I could possibly square belief in a good and almighty God with the fact of living in an often evil world.'

Now, I suppose that if the Bible never mentioned the problem of evil—its origins, its definition, its judgement and its cure—then the unbeliever might just have a point. But as anyone who makes it to the end of the first three chapters of the book will be aware, it does indeed mention these things: its origins—stemming from the hearts of the first man and woman and spilling over into their actions (Genesis 3:1–6); its definition—rebellion against the Creator (Genesis 3:11–13); its judgement—physical, spiritual and eternal death (Genesis 2:17); and its cure—the promise of a Saviour (Genesis 3:15).

Yes, we Christians are aware of what many unbelievers think about these passages, but all the same, it would be well to consider the total lack of answers given by atheistic humanism to the problem of evil before dismissing the Christian answer out of hand. Are there any proper answers given by atheistic humanism? If there are, I was blissfully unaware of them, so rather than shaking Alex's hand and bowing out gracefully from the conversation, I soldiered on and began to answer his objection as best I could:

'I was wondering how long it would be before that particular question came up.'

'Well, it does kind of throw a bit of a spanner into your works, doesn't it?' he said tartly. 'I mean, it doesn't fit in very well with all that usual Christian claptrap about the God of peace and love, does it?'

'It fits in perfectly with it,' I replied. 'But before I can answer your question, I need to first clear something up. Let me ask you a question, Alex: You and I, are we free men, or two machines talking to one another?'

'What a bizarre question!' he said. 'I think I'm a free man. I can't answer for you, though.'

'I think the same,' I replied. 'Okay, now say I suddenly pull a knife on you: Who is responsible, me or God?'

'Even stranger than the last question!' said Alex, looking at me as if I had lost my marbles. 'You, I suppose. Why do you ask?'

'I ask it purely to clear up one particular issue that I think unbelievers often confuse. And that is the origin and the responsibility of evil. When unbelievers say things like, "If God is so good, why does he allow evil?" it sounds to me as if they are pointing the finger of blame at God for the evil that men do. As if it were somehow God that did it. Take the Holocaust. Many have used this as a reason for turning to rank unbelief. But does the blame lie with Hitler or with God?'

'Look, I'm not blaming God for Hitler's crimes,' replied Alex. 'All I'm doing is questioning how a "good" God allowed Hitler to commit such crimes.'

'Mmm,' I said. 'It still sounds to me like God is getting some of the blame for it. Or am I misrepresenting you?'

'Yes, you are,' replied Alex. 'I didn't even remotely say I blamed him for causing the Holocaust.'

'No, but you do blame him for not preventing it, don't you?'

'Well no, because I don't believe he exists to be able to prevent it,' replied Alex.

'Okay,' I replied, 'so I think I'm right in saying that with regard to the origin of and responsibility for evil, your unbelief therefore leaves you with little choice but to agree with me that the following statements are true:

- It is men and women who commit evil, not God.
- Evil must stem from men and women's hearts, not God's.
- Evil is therefore men and women's responsibility, not God's.

'Right?'

'Right.'

'Well, now that we've established that the origin of and responsibility for evil is man's and man's alone, it's time to look at the definition. So you want me to tell you how God allows evil in the world. Fine, but can you tell me what ES we are using?'

He gave no reply, only a rather funny look.

'ES—ethical standard,' I answered. 'You have said that there is evil in the world, but I just wanted to know what exactly you meant by that and by which ethical standard you are judging what is and what isn't evil.'

'Oh, come on,' he said. 'There are murders, genocide, rapes and all sorts of things going on all the time. Are you denying that these things are evil?'

'Not at all. I just wanted to define our terms before I begin answering the question, just to make sure that we are in the same ballpark. You see, one problem we have is that my ethical standard,' I said, pointing to the Bible, 'goes a little bit beyond murders, genocide and rape in its definition of what evil is. As well as these things, and in no particular order, it says that the following things are also evil: denying the true God, lying, theft, covetousness, hatred, idolatry, adultery, dishonouring parents, deceitfulness, ingratitude, homosexuality, bitterness, divorce, unfaithfulness, strife, anger against another without a cause, blasphemy, drunkenness, withholding good from others, fornication, divination, pride, gossiping, lust, envy, and so on. So if you're asking me to tell you how God can allow evil in the world, I first wanted to know whether we are singing from the same ethical hymnsheet and if you would include all of these things.'

'No, I wouldn't include all of them,' he replied. 'Especially not things like blasphemy. How can it be evil to blaspheme something that I don't believe in?'

'Well, this is the whole point,' I replied. 'The reason you don't believe that blasphemy is evil, and I guess a number of other things on the list I mentioned, is because you don't really have an absolute ethical standard by which to judge things. So all your views of what is and what isn't evil will be completely arbitrary, and you can no more say that murder is right or wrong than you can say that blasphemy is right or wrong.'

'Well, it's pretty obvious that murder is wrong, isn't it?' he exclaimed in a rather irritated voice. 'And it's not very obvious that blasphemy is wrong, is it?'

'Isn't it?' I said, sounding surprised. 'Go on.'

'Oh, come on!' he replied. 'I don't have to believe what is written in your book to see that murder is wrong. It's as plain as the nose on your face!'

'Well, if I really believed that you and I were nothing but a couple of bundles of assembled atoms, I wouldn't think that this was so obvious at all. On the contrary, if I truly believed this, I would rather think that it was pretty obvious that "murdering" people was neither wrong nor right. It would be as neutral as any other act involving bundles of atoms—like eating a bar of chocolate, for example. And the consequences arising from both actions would be roughly the same.'

'What do you mean by that?' he asked.

'Well, let me put it this way,' I replied. 'Suppose we lived in the godless universe you claim to believe in, where we are all annihilated at death. Say I decided to kill you. In the grand scheme of things, the act would have precisely no consequences whatsoever; you would simply go from being animate dust to inanimate dust. And as for me, I would face no ultimate justice for my "crime" and would myself go from being animate dust to inanimate dust in due course as well. In terms of consequences, in the universe you claim to believe in, there would be no more ultimate difference between one of us killing the other and eating a bar of chocolate; both acts would be entirely insignificant.'

'Absolute rubbish!' cried Alex. 'All you're doing is just trying to turn the argument on its head to avoid having to confront the real issue, which is how it is that your supposedly good and omnipotent God appears to be utterly impotent when it comes to dealing with evil!'

'Not at all,' I replied. 'I just wanted to establish what exactly you meant by "evil", since it appears to me that you have no absolute ethical standard by which to judge what is good and what is evil. But no matter, I'll try to answer the question on your terms. Let me ask you, do you perceive yourself to be a perfect man, who has never done, said or even thought anything even remotely evil in his life?'

'Of course not,' he replied. 'But what's that got to do with anything?'

'Quite a lot really, Alex,' I said. 'You see, the question "If there is a God, why does he allow evil in the world?" could be genuinely asked only by someone who was completely free from evil. But you have just admitted that you are not such a person. Therefore, by asking the question "If God exists, why does he allow evil in the world?" what you are doing is inviting God to come and destroy you from off the face of the earth.'

It was clear from his face that he didn't really follow what I was getting at, so I went on:

'I assume from your question that you think that God, if he is as good and as omnipotent as I am claiming, ought to do something about all the evil in the world. Agreed?'

He nodded his assent.

'And I further assume that by "doing something about the evil that exists" you mean that he should rid the world of it. Agreed?'

Again he nodded his head.

'Well then,' I continued, 'if God ought to destroy all evil—and you have admitted that you are imperfect, sometimes doing, saying or thinking evil—then does it not follow that you would be one of the ones that God "ought to do something about"?'

'Look, there's a bit of a difference between, say, having an argument with your wife and killing someone,' he said in exasperation.

'Well, of course there is,' I replied. 'But are you saying that because a great evil is done, it somehow turns a lesser evil into a good? Murderers are bad, and so because of their acts we—the wife-arguers—must be good! Surely God must be so pleased with us for just arguing with our wives rather than killing them! But let me ask you this, Alex: What if God, instead of playing along with this little game of ethical relativism we have invented, marks all of us—the wife-arguers and the murderers—down as bad and, rather than seeing good and bad, just sees bad and worse?'

He thought about this for a moment but said nothing. I pondered for a moment or two how amazing it is that unbelievers cannot see the contradiction in their position here. They begin by asking how the God of the Bible can be good when he allows evil. Now you might think that if someone is going to question the God of the Bible's justice and judgement, out of sheer courtesy the God of the Bible should be allowed to answer this question using his ethical standard, wouldn't you?

But no, what Alex and Co. are really interested in doing is haranguing the God of the Bible, not for failing to deal with things he defines as evil, but for not doing something about the things that Alex and Co. define as evil. Isn't it obvious, though, that if he does do something about evil, it will not be done according to Alex and Co.'s definition of evil but rather his own?

I gave Alex the following illustration of how this works.

Imagine a schoolroom with a teacher standing at the front of the class. He tells the class that he has to go and speak to another teacher and that he will be back in ten minutes or so. Before leaving the room, he tells the children to remain seated and to open their workbooks and continue working their way through the exercises. Now, when he comes back, he finds a third of the class throwing paper around the room; another third of them standing on the desks ripping their exercise books up; and the final third over by the windows, squirting lighter fluid on the curtains and setting them on fire. You get the picture?

Now I'm sure that everyone would agree that of all the three groups, the behaviour of the third group was by far the worst and deserved the greatest punishment. And I'm equally sure everyone would agree that of all the three groups, the behaviour of the first group was the least worst and deserved the least severe punishment.

But would you agree that even though there was a clear difference in the levels of behaviour among the groups, it was still the case that all three groups had disobeyed their teacher and so were deserving of punishment, albeit to differing degrees? So would it surprise you to know that when the first group were questioned about their behaviour, rather than admitting that he had indeed disobeyed the teacher's instruction and so was deserving of punishment, each child pointed the finger at the behaviour of the second and third groups and asked the teacher why he didn't do something about their behaviour?

Well, each of us is like the first group. We are all looking at the behaviour of others and excusing ourselves on the basis of their bad behaviour. But it just won't do in the eyes of God. Just as there wasn't a single child in that classrooom who was innocent of disobeying the teacher's command, neither is there a single inhabitant of the earth who is innocent of disobeying God's commands. Yes, there are degrees of bad behaviour, but not one of us can genuinely claim that we have done, said or even thought no evil. As the apostle Paul puts it: 'There is none righteous, no, not one' (Romans 3:10).

So oughtn't we to be very careful when asking God to come and deal with all the evil in the world? Because if he actually took us at our word and did what we were asking, we would all be destroyed. Not just Adolf Hitler and Joseph Stalin, but all of us. As it says in Psalm 130:3: 'If thou, LORD, shouldest mark iniquities, O Lord, who shall stand?'

Alex pondered all I had said for a few moments before giving his reply.

'There are a couple of important differences between your classroom example and the real world. Firstly, in your illustration, presumably the teacher did actually deal with the situation when he came back. Whereas in the world you and I live in, this rarely, if ever, happens. Murderers often escape justice. Many rapists and thieves get away with it. Power-hungry tyrants oppress people and get away with it. People commit genocide and get away with it. Nothing is done about these things.

'And secondly, in your example, presumably the third group were dealt with far more severely than the first group. Whereas in the real world, the fact is that the worst offenders—the dictators and the tyrants—seem to be able to do what they want while the poor people they rule over are punished. How on earth you can square these things with your "almighty" and "just" God is beyond my comprehension.'

'Well, before I attempt to answer this,' I replied, 'tell me, Alex, do you actually care about these great evils you have mentioned, or are you just using them as a stick with which to beat down God and to justify your unbelief?'

'Well, of course I care!' he said incredulously.

'Well, please forgive me if I am misjudging you personally,' I said, 'but my experience of how unbelievers generally approach the subject of evil suggests that there is often an element of disingenuousness about it. One minute they can be expressing horror at outrages happening around the world, and the next minute they can be telling jokes about the same events. I've heard people telling or laughing at jokes about abortion, murder, rape, kidnapping, child molesters, 9/11 and yes, even about the Holocaust. No subject is out of bounds. And yet, at other times, I've seen the very same people wringing their hands in horror at these things and asking how there could ever be a God who would allow such things to happen. Ever laughed at one of these jokes?'

He said nothing, but I fancied that he looked a little ashamed.

'No need to hide it,' I said. 'I freely admit to you that I laughed at such jokes before I became a Christian and started taking the problem of evil seriously for the first time, beginning with the most potent evil that I know of—that which is in my own heart. But assuming that you are genuinely horrified by the evil of which you speak and also that you are genuinely perplexed by the fact that the world looks as it does, I suppose I'd better tell you how I can square the fact that wicked acts often go unpunished with the idea of an omnipotent God, hadn't I?

'I believe you are making two mistakes here:

'The first is the assumption that wicked acts really do go unpunished. You are beginning from the entirely naturalistic presupposition that this life is all there is, and if that were the case, then it would indeed be true that wicked acts do go unpunished. But you forget that a universe created by God would not be founded according to your naturalistic assumptions and that this life would not be the only life there is. In other words, in criticizing God for the fact that wickedness prevails and is unpunished in this life, all you are doing is imposing your own naturalistic presuppositions on God and then criticizing him for not operating within your parameters. The words "cake" and "eat it" spring to mind.

'But the Bible makes it abundantly clear that, ultimately, God will not let wickedness go unpunished, even if it appears that it does in this life. Take Psalm 98, for example,' I said, turning to the page in my Bible. 'Verse 9 says, "With righteousness shall he [God] judge the world, and the people with equity." When is he going to do this? Now? No, not now, but at the end of each individual's life—"It is appointed unto men once to die, but after this the judgment" (Hebrews 9:27)—and in the judgement at the end of the world—"And I saw the dead, small and great, stand before God; and the books were opened: and another book was opened, which is the book of life: and the dead were judged out of those things which were written in the books, according to their works" (Revelation 20:12).

'And this brings me to your second mistake, which is that in denying the existence of God, you are effectively denying the only hope you have of ever seeing justice done. With my worldview, I have a sure and certain hope that every single piece of wickedness ever committed on this earth will be punished. But what is bizarre about your position is that, even if you really do care about the evils you have mentioned and you really do want to see justice for all these things, realistically you have no hope whatsoever of seeing this realized. How is the godless universe going to mete out justice? You've admitted yourself that sometimes what you define as good triumphs, but sometimes it doesn't. Sometimes what you define as evil is punished, but sometimes it isn't. But whether or not you get a little justice on this earth is fairly irrelevant in any case, as everything will be annihilated in due course anyway—oppressors and the oppressed, murderers and the murdered, rapists and the raped—all will die, and what will you be left with? No justice, no recompense, no nothing. Seems to me that you have just two options if you really followed your own worldview to its logical conclusion: either you would sink into depression at the realization of the full ghastliness of it and eventually kill yourself, or you would end up making jokes about it.'

Alex chewed on what I had said for a while before turning back to the basic question of why evil exists.

'Look,' he said, 'you can bang on all you like about how God is allegedly going to do this and do that to those who commit evil acts, but you still haven't explained why God—if he exists—actually allows these things to happen in the first place. If he is good, he ought never to have allowed evil in the first place. And if he is omniscient and omnipotent, then it ought to be a doddle for him to stop it, shouldn't it? But as evil clearly exists, it suggests that he cannot be good, omniscient or omnipotent. Wasn't it Epicurus who put it like this:

Is God willing to prevent evil, but not able?
Then he is not omnipotent.
Is he able, but not willing?
Then he is malevolent.
Is he both able and willing?
Then whence cometh evil?
Is he neither able nor willing?
Then why call him God?[1]

'So what's the answer? Explain to me why the almighty God cannot seem to stop these things.'

'Yes, it was Epicurus,' I said. 'How do I answer his seemingly clever little riddle? Well, I'll try, but I think to do so, it is best to put it in the context of a real situation. So let's take the simplest example of the kind of evil you are talking about, say, Cain and Abel.'

'A couple of fictional characters,' interjected Alex.

'Well, for the purposes of this illustration, it is unimportant that you think that,' I said. 'If you want to imagine another couple of brothers where one kills the other, be my guest. Call them Colin and Albert, if you like. Okay, so you and Epicurus will both say, "If God is both omniscient and good, how and why would he ever have allowed Cain to have such a wicked thought in his head? Surely he should have foreseen it and prevented it." But the simple answer to that is that Cain, as a man created in the image of God, was given the ability to choose between two types of behaviour: loving his brother and hating his brother.

'You and Epicurus will then probably ask why God allowed him the choice of hating his brother. Well, again the answer is a simple one. If Cain hadn't been given this choice, then he never could have truly loved Abel. Rather, Cain would have simply been programmed to "love" Abel—whatever that means—and so his love for him would have been purely mechanical, which is not love at all. It is only because I know what pain is like that I know that I prefer being without pain. And it is only if I am given the choice between love and hate that I can truly love.

'But what of the act of murder itself, and what God should have done? Both you and Epicurus will say, "If God is omnipotent, why didn't he stop Cain from killing his brother?" Now on these terms—that God should have intervened to stop Cain's wickedness—as Cain was about to strike, God essentially had three choices before him: he could simply have prevented Cain from doing it, either by natural or miraculous means; he could simply have destroyed Cain before he did his deed; or he could have taken Cain and "reprogrammed" him like a computer so that he never again had such a thought in his head.

'But with each of these "solutions" there is an insurmountable problem. The problem with the first option—preventing Cain doing the deed—is that Cain's heart would have remained unchanged, and he would simply have looked for another opportunity to carry out his crime.

This is not to say that God does not use such means to prevent much more evil in the world from occurring than actually does occur, but even so he only prevents evil acts from occurring without necessarily altering the state of evildoers' hearts.

'The problem with the second option—destroying Cain—is that not only would Cain need to be destroyed, but Abel too, because he also was guilty of his own sins before God. And the problem with the third option—reprogramming Cain—is that Cain would have lost his free will, and therefore the very thing that defined his humanity would have been destroyed and he would have become just another animal. With the first, the sin would be harboured within Cain's heart to be brought out into the open another day. With the second, all humanity would be wiped off the face of the earth, because all—not just the Cains and the Hitlers of this world—are guilty before God. And with the third, Cain would no longer be made in the image of God but would now be nothing more than a programmed machine. But whichever option God chose, humanity would effectively be dead.'

'So instead he chose the fourth way, which was "just do nothing"!' said Alex.

'No,' I responded, 'that's just where you're wrong! The option he chose was not "just do nothing", it was very much "do something". But whatever that something was, it needed to deal with the problem of the evil in men's hearts, not just by temporarily preventing evil, but by banishing it for ever. It also needed to solve the problem of preserving life, and it needed to preserve man's essential humanity. So how did he do it?'

'I expect you're going to tell me it's something to do with Jesus Christ and the cross of Calvary, aren't you?'

'Yes, I am, and I make no apologies for doing so,' I replied firmly. 'Because this is the only solution under the sun that truly deals with the problem of evil while at the same time overcoming the three problems I have mentioned. Why? If you really want evil to cease, then you must accept that all evil must be judged—and this includes your own. And if after hearing this you still want evil to cease, you must hope that God can find a way of destroying your own evil while not destroying you. And if after hearing this you still want evil to cease, you must hope that he can find a way of doing this without interfering with your humanity and turning you into a mere robot that does good because it is programmed to rather than because it truly desires to do so. Well, in Christ and in him alone all these conditions are fulfilled. For those who trust in him, sin is judged, their life is spared and their humanity is not compromised. And so, for what it's worth, here is my answer to Epicurus' riddle:

Is God willing to prevent evil, but not able?
He is perfectly able, but in his time, not yours, Epicurus.
Is he able, but not willing?
He is perfectly willing to do so, but using his method, not yours, Epicurus.
Is he both able and willing?
He is both able and willing, but he must do so in such a way that changes the heart, maintains the life and preserves the humanity of evildoers such as you and me, Epicurus.
Is he neither able nor willing?
His ability will be finally seen at the end of time, when he destroys all evil for good.
His willingness was seen when his Son took the place of evildoers on the cross.
But are you able and willing to accept his remedy for all evil, including your own, or will you let him come and destroy you when he finally banishes evil for ever, Epicurus?

'Okay, I admit it's not quite as brief nor as catchy as the original, but it does at least provide an answer to Epicurus' riddle, don't you think? Or do you think that Epicurus would have reacted badly against the revelation that he was as much a part of the problem of evil as anyone else, and that he wasn't quite as good and as moral as he maybe liked to think?'

'Good and moral?' replied Alex. 'Of course, you're going to tell me that you can only be good if you believe in God! Well, I beg to differ. You don't need to believe in God to be moral.'

Notes

1 http://thinkexist.com/quotation/is-god-willing-to-prevent-evil-but-not-able-then/411189. html.

Objection 4: You don't need to believe in God to be moral

It was coffee time! The lady with the trolley of food and drink had reached us down the aisle, and when she asked us if we wanted anything, Alex very kindly offered to buy me a coffee. It turned out that we both drank it black with no sugar, and so I remarked wryly to Alex that this was the fifth similarity I had discovered between us today, along with our age, lunch, reading material and the fact that we were both married with children.

Alex replied equally wryly that surely the fact that we were both travelling home on the 14:15 from Waterloo meant we actually had six things in common. We both had a bit of a laugh about this and sat for a few moments sipping our coffees, musing on the possibility of finding ten similarities before the end of the journey. Alex, for his part, remarked that we appeared to have the same number of hands and feet. For my part, I remembered that we were both due to have sausages for dinner that night, bringing the total number of similarities right up to eight. Unfortunately, we never quite made it to the magic number ten as the conversation then took a detour, and before we knew it we had arrived back at our discussion of Life, the Universe and Everything, this time honing in on the issue of morality.

'Look, Alex,' I said. 'Before we go on to this, I really think we ought to clear up what it is we mean by being moral. Do you believe that right exists and that wrong exists?'

'Well, of course I do!' he said.

'And where do you think they come from?' I asked him.

'Evolution,' he replied immediately. 'Morality has evolved as man has evolved.'

'I'm not quite sure I understand what you are saying,' I replied. 'Do you mean that morality itself has evolved, or do you mean that human understanding of morality has evolved?'

He looked at me a little blankly, so I put it to him that claiming that morality has evolved as man has evolved might mean any one of three things:

1. It might mean that morality itself has evolved, so that what was really and truly moral, say, a thousand years ago, is no longer really and truly moral now.
2. It might mean that morality has always been an absolute, but humans didn't in the past understand or adhere to it, and as time has gone on they are coming closer and closer to true morality.
3. Or it might mean that morality is literally defined by humans themselves, and therefore whatsoever men decree as being moral at any given time is really and truly moral.

'Whichever one of these lines of thought you take,' I said, 'I think that you have some serious and insurmountable problems. Taking the first possibility—that morality itself has evolved—the problem with this, Alex, is that it actually destroys the very concept of morality. Morality—if that term means anything at all—must be a fixed concept which means the same today as it did yesterday and will tomorrow, or it means nothing at all. To say that morality itself is evolving is a bit like saying that "sadness" is evolving or that "triangles" are evolving or that the colour "blue" is evolving. If you followed this line of thinking with regard to morality, you would be forced to concede that anything which we call "immoral" today—say, the rituals of ancient pagans burning their children alive in the fire to their "gods"—was not necessarily immoral back then, and that anything we call "moral" today may not necessarily be so tomorrow.

'As for the second possibility—that morality is an absolute and as time has gone on man has got closer and closer to true morality—there are three problems with this: the first is that you cannot tell me where that absolute came from; the second is that you cannot tell me what that absolute is; and the third is that the twentieth century—probably the bloodiest of all centuries—ought to put paid to any claims that man is getting any closer to true morality.

'As for the third possibility—that morality is literally defined by humans themselves—I suppose that if all men were in agreement on what is moral and observed it consistently, you might have a case. But of course they don't agree. The Romans thought it harmless fun to throw Christians into the lions' den and watch them as they were torn to shreds. The Nazi and Soviet regimes thought it was perfectly acceptable to work, starve and torture certain people to their deaths. They didn't seem to see any harm in it, and so if men define morality, then what they did was perfectly moral.

'Playing the "evolution card" to explain morality might seem to be plausible on the surface, but dig a little deeper and I'm afraid it just doesn't stack up. Whereas if you start with the biblical proposition that morality has been given by God—that men are created in the image of God and that the moral law is written on their hearts—then all the problems I just mentioned with your explanation simply disappear.'

'Hardly,' he replied instantly. 'If the moral law is really written on men's hearts, then how come they are in such disagreement on moral issues? How do you explain the pagans slaughtering their children or the Romans killing Christians or the Nazis gassing Jews?'

'Well, let me ask you one simple question. When the pagans or the Romans or the Nazis did what they did, did they know that it was really wrong?'

'Not according to you,' he replied. 'You said a moment ago that they all thought it was perfectly acceptable.'

'That's not exactly what I asked,' I countered. 'I am not asking if they *thought* they were doing wrong. I am asking if they *knew* they were doing wrong.'

He asked me what the difference was, so I put it like this: that it is entirely possible for someone to commit a great evil, all the while convincing themselves that what they are doing is right, and yet deep down knowing full well that what they are doing is wrong. This is a fundamentally crucial point of human nature to grasp; if you fail to accept it, it effectively means that you cannot ever legitimately blame anyone for any wrongdoing. Why? Because in condemning wrongdoing you are assuming that the person or persons you are condemning knew that what they were doing was wrong but that they deliberately and wilfully ignored what they knew to be right. If the Neros, the Hitlers and the Stalins of this world really weren't aware that what they were doing was wrong, we would have no right to condemn them for what they did, as they could in no way be said to be responsible for their actions. Rather, our attitude to them could only be one of pity for them that they weren't able to see that what they were doing was wrong.

'But I take it you don't believe that, do you?' I asked him.

'Of course I don't,' he said.

'Which brings me back to the answer to your question: How can I claim that morality is written on the hearts of men when men are in disagreement on moral issues and when they commit horrendous atrocities for "the greater good"? The fact that you are able to condemn regimes of terror shows beyond any reasonable doubt that you believe that the perpetrators of such crimes had the same basic understanding of morality as you, which in turn suggests that the moral law is indeed written into our very being. But how, then, do men come to commit hideous atrocities despite having this basic moral understanding? Simple—they completely and wilfully ignore it, just as the Bible says.'

'Okay, so let's say that morality is a universal absolute,' Alex replied, 'and let's say that all men have some understanding of it but are able to ignore it. I don't have a problem with this. Perhaps I'm not able to fully explain how this happened, but maybe one day humans will have a better understanding of these things. Nevertheless, however we got our morality, I still maintain that you can be a moral person without believing in God. I know loads of people who don't believe in God and who are perfectly moral.'

'Perfectly moral?' I said with a smile on my face. 'That's a pretty big claim. On what absolute basis are you judging these people, and—I assume—yourself to be perfectly moral?'

'Look, I don't believe in God, but I've never done any harm to anyone,' he replied a bit sharply. 'If that doesn't constitute morality, then I don't know what does.'

'Harm?' I said with a note of surprise. 'So is that the absolute value you are using to judge whether you and others are moral?'

'Yes,' he said, 'it is.'

'Well, quite apart from the fact that this is irrelevant to the issue of morality, is it even strictly true? You mentioned a while ago about arguing with your wife—at least I assume that this was something drawn from your own personal experience. So is it really true to say that you have never done any harm to anyone?'

'Yes,' he affirmed. 'We may have our ups and downs, but we forgive each other and we're still together. So where's the harm?'

'Whether there is or isn't any is debatable,' I replied. 'But nevertheless, it is a point which is pretty irrelevant in any discussion of morality. I suppose that a suicide bomber whose explosives fail to detonate could legitimately claim that he hasn't done anyone any harm. Whereas the judge who sentences the attempted suicide bomber to prison and therefore to a loss of liberty could not legitimately claim that he hasn't done anyone any harm. But would you say that the attempted suicide bomber is the more moral of the two?'

'No,' he said.

'Exactly,' I replied, 'and that's because the issue of harm is largely irrelevant to the issue of morality. Apart from anything, harm can be an entirely relative concept, if extricated from an overarching moral law. What one person considers harm—say, daubing graffiti on a subway wall—might constitute "harmless fun" to another.

'But the biggest trouble with this way of thinking is that it mistakes actions and consequences as being the same thing. Saying something hurtful to your wife is an action, but it is not necessarily the case that it will result in a bad consequence. For example, she may not hear you use some derogatory comment about her, or maybe she does but then she forgives you. Either way, no bad consequences arise from the comment. But does this mean that your action was right? No! The fact that a good consequence follows hateful words is neither here nor there. It is the action, the words or the thoughts, that is the determinant as to whether something is moral, and it is simply untrue to assume that because no harmful consequences arise from it that this somehow constitutes morality.'

I carried on by pointing out that it is entirely possible for a man to live the whole of his life full of bad thoughts and intentions and yet never carry any of these things out and so never do any 'harm' to anyone else. But is the man moral? It is also possible for a man to live the whole of his life never doing any 'harm' to anyone else, but in all that time he may never do any good to anyone at all. Take Scrooge. He could probably have claimed, 'I've never done any harm to anyone else.' But what was Dickens's point? Scrooge was a selfish miser who only ever thought of himself.

I could tell by Alex's slightly disconcerted look that this was the first time he had had his 'no harm' badge of morality challenged, and it was several moments before he pulled his thoughts together.

'Look, when I said that I hadn't done any harm to anyone else, I didn't just mean that I hadn't murdered anyone or that I don't sit in my house counting my money and harbouring hatred for other people in my heart. I did actually mean that I have done some positive good to others.'

'I don't doubt it,' I answered. 'But even this does not constitute what I, as a Christian, understand morality to mean. What you're really saying is that your good actions outweigh your bad. Right?'

'I suppose,' he replied.

'Then we have reached the crux of the whole argument: your idea of morality works like a set of scales. Over here on the right,' I said, gesturing with my hand, 'are your good works. And over here on the left are your bad works. And you would presumably suggest to me that the right hand is heavier than the left. Right?'

'I think so,' he said.

I put it to Alex that this is the basic position that everybody naturally has when thinking about themselves in the context of morality. There are, however, three major problems with thinking along these lines:

1. Even on our own terms, this thinking is flawed because we are judging ourselves and, frankly, anyone can score well when judged by their own standards of morality. If we transgress our standard, we only have to move the goalposts, change the standard and we are still a 'good person'.

2. Anyone judging himself is bound to overlook many, if not all, of his transgressions against his own standards. All the hateful, proud and lustful thoughts we have had will be overlooked. All the unkind words, deceit and the lies we have spoken will be ignored. And all the many horrible things we have done will be swept under the carpet.

3. But as if these problems weren't bad enough, the third is even more fundamental to the question of morality. For this definition of morality—that our good actions outweigh our bad actions—is utterly relative and therefore renders the notion of morality meaningless. The Christian definition of morality, on the other hand, is infinitely higher. It is an absolute. It sets an absolute standard, and it allows for no breaches of this absolute standard. That is why Jesus said in the Sermon on the Mount, 'Be ye therefore perfect, even as your Father which is in heaven is perfect' (Matthew 5:48). His idea of morality wasn't relativistic and individualistic; rather, he preached that true morality is a flawless, eternal absolute, and so all who would describe themselves as truly moral beings must themselves measure up to this flawless, eternal absolute.

'Flawless, eternal absolute?' Alex laughed, shaking his head. 'You know, that's exactly the problem I have with you Christians. You think yourselves to be so much better than everyone else.'

'If that's really what you think, then I have to say that your understanding of Christianity is way, way off the mark. Why on earth do you think we put our trust in a Saviour to take away our sins? Because we are perfect? Why on earth do you think we fall to our knees each day and ask God to forgive us our sins? Because we perceive ourselves to be good and holy people?

'The truth is exactly the opposite. We do so because when we stop measuring ourselves against our own relativistic and movable standard of morality and begin to measure ourselves against the flawless, eternal absolute—that is, the moral law of God and Jesus Christ who gave and kept that law—we realize that we are anything but perfect. Rather, we see what vile, immoral wretches we are, guilty of sin, worthy of death but eternally thankful for the mercy God has offered us to save us from his wrath.'

'It sounds like a case of false humility from where I'm sitting, coupled with an inability to cope with the psychological feelings of guilt we all get from time to time.'

'Oh, the guilt is real, I can assure you of that,' I replied. 'And as for false humility, if that's really what you think, there's not a great deal I can do about it—but tell me, have you never heard the parable of the Pharisee and the publican?'

He told me he was vaguely familiar with it, so I opened my Bible and read the whole parable:

And he spake this parable unto certain which trusted in themselves that they were righteous, and despised others: Two men went up into the temple to pray; the one a Pharisee, and the other a publican. The Pharisee stood and prayed thus with himself, God, I thank thee, that I am not as other men are, extortioners, unjust, adulterers, or even as this publican. I fast twice in the week, I give tithes of all that I possess. And the publican, standing afar off, would not lift up so much as his eyes unto heaven, but smote upon his breast, saying, God be merciful to me a sinner. I tell you, this man went down to his house justified rather than the other: for every one that exalteth himself shall be abased; and he that humbleth himself shall be exalted (Luke 18:9–14).

'I hate to say it, Alex, but though you might not believe in God like the Pharisee, though you might not go to "church" like the Pharisee and though you might not pray like the Pharisee, aren't you in exactly the same position as the Pharisee? You might like to think that we Christians are the ones who say, "Thank God we're not like other men", but the truth is, one of the fundamentals of our belief is that we are like other men: not good, but corrupt sinners all. Whereas you have told me, on the basis of an entirely relativistic idea of morality, that you are perfectly moral.'

'So what you are saying is that we are completely incapable of doing good, of helping others and of loving others,' was his rather sardonic reply.

'No, I am not saying that at all. As a creature made in the image of God, even though that image is fallen, of course we are still capable of doing "moral things". But this is quite different from "being moral". You started off by saying that you don't need to believe in God to be moral. Well, the issue here is not belief as such, but rather whether you could ever even be moral or legitimately claim to be moral if there really is no God. And the fact is that if you truly deny the existence of God, you find yourself caught in a relativistic cul-de-sac from which you cannot escape: you have effectively denied any claim you might have that ultimate and absolute truth exists, which means that you have effectively denied any claim you might have that absolute morality exists, which means that you have effectively denied any claim you might have to be a moral being, because not only is your standard relativistic and subjective, but so, by extension, are your actions.

'In which case, why on earth should anyone attach any meaning to or believe there is any truth in your words when you say, "You don't need to believe in God to be moral"? No God—no absolute truth—no absolute morality—no absolute personal morality. Only the relativistic, subjective claims of trying to prove our own goodness without an absolute standard of morality and truth to measure it against.'

'Truth?' questioned Alex. 'Tell me, what exactly do you mean by that? What is truth?'

Objection 5: What is truth?

We sat there for the next few minutes in silence, just looking out the window. We were passing by the edge of a forest, and I must say that it looked stunning, decked out in glorious shades of autumn greens, yellows, golden browns and reds. I think both of us got lost in the beauty of it all for a few moments, which I was thankful for after the heat of our discussion during the previous few minutes. It was good to just sit there and take it all in, and I was glad for both our sakes that we were able to take a breather. But as we left the forest behind, I was prompted by Alex back to his last question, and my thoughts returned to our discussion once more.

'It's funny—not really "ha-ha" funny, more ironic funny—but probably without even realizing it, you have just quoted from the Bible. Were you aware of it?'

Alex shook his head and shrugged his shoulders, indicating that he wasn't.

'Not only this,' I went on, 'but the quotation comes from the lips of one of the most notorious men in all history. Any guesses?'

After he guessed wrongly at Judas Iscariot, I informed him that it was actually Pontius Pilate. I then opened my Bible and read the passage from the eighteenth chapter of John's Gospel, where Jesus declares that everyone who hears his voice is of the truth. Pilate responds by saying, 'What is truth?' before immediately walking out. It is not explicitly stated in the passage how Pilate asked this question, but the fact that he walked out straight away without hearing a reply suggests that the question was at best flippant and disingenuous, and at worst downright sneering. At any rate, what is clear is that Pilate didn't believe that there was any such thing as absolute truth.

'It's interesting,' I continued, 'but I remember that when I was an unbeliever, I couldn't really see an awful lot wrong with Pilate. I mean, just what was he to do? It's early in the morning, and there he is with this man, Jesus, whom he knows almost nothing about and for whom he cares even less, and there's a crowd beneath him, screaming and baying for blood like a pack of beasts. And though he seems fairly keen to release Jesus, saying several times to the mob that he finds no fault with him, the wolves won't be placated. So in the end, he doesn't seem to have an awful lot of choice in the matter.

'Okay, you might say he is a bit of a coward, but unlike Judas who betrayed Jesus and the mob who wanted Jesus executed, surely we can have some sympathy with old Pilate, can't we? He just found himself caught in a bad situation. He had better things to do with his time and he just wanted out, didn't he? Nothing too wrong with that, is there?

'But looking at it as a believer, I can now see two things: firstly, Pilate's actions in allowing Christ to be crucified were directly linked to his dismissive question "What is truth?" If he had had any concept of absolute truth, he would have found the idea of handing a man he knew to be innocent over to the mob utterly reprehensible and would have done all he could as governor to protect him. But because he didn't believe in truth, being a relativist to the core, he was entirely capable of declaring a man to be wholly innocent, only to hand him over to be crucified a few moments later.

'And the second thing I can now see is with regard to myself. It was my disregard for the truth, my own relativism—just like that of Pilate—which blinded me from seeing his enormous sin in allowing the mob to have their way and crucify the innocent. It also blinded me from seeing my enormous sin in thinking little of this.'

These last sentences didn't go down particularly well with Alex, and he protested at what he saw as the implication that anyone who didn't hold to what I believe to be the truth would hand innocent men over to be executed. I pointed out to him that I wasn't necessarily saying that anyone who fails to believe in what I believe to be the truth would have done exactly what Pilate did; merely that without believing in transcendent truth, it is at least a distinct possibility.

'The point is this,' I continued. 'You start off with Pilate's question, where you deny the existence of objective, transcendent truth, and where do you end up? Anywhere that takes your fancy! Perhaps you would have defended Jesus if you had been there. Or perhaps you would have done exactly what Pilate did. On the basis of his own relativism, the "What is truth?" man can end up anywhere he likes.

'Now, there are many problems with this, but perhaps the most obvious is that if you get more than one person living in a society—and that usually seems to be the way—this is a recipe for chaos. A society with one man making up his own truth might just about get along okay for a while, but just imagine what would happen in a nation where millions of people all hold their own versions of the truth. No, wait! You don't even have to imagine; just look around you at the society you live in. It is fast becoming the epitome of the existentialist, relativistic "What is truth?" society where—as it says in the commentary on the depravity of the nation of Israel at the end of the book of Judges—"every man did that which was right in his own eyes" (Judges 21:25).'

To illustrate the point, I asked him whether he had ever seen those adverts on London buses, funded by Richard Dawkins and the British Humanist Association, which said: 'There's probably no God, so stop worrying and enjoy yourself.'

Alex replied that he was familiar with them, and added for good measure that they had probably helped a lot of people over their delusion.

I agreed with him. The adverts had prompted the Trinitarian Bible Society to respond with their own series of adverts based on Psalm 14:1—'The fool hath said in his heart, There is no God'—and this had led to a good number of people requesting Bibles and had also prompted many conversations with others who had become concerned for their state before God after seeing the ads. But as this wasn't exactly the 'good' he was referring to, I asked him what he meant.

'I'm sure it would have made a few people think,' he said. 'You know, those people who've spent their whole lives in self-denial because of some make-believe threat that they're going to get judged for enjoying themselves.'

'Okay,' I said, 'forgive me if I'm wrong, but what the advert was essentially saying is this: there's no God, so you're free to do your own thing. Right?'

'Exactly,' said Alex.

'Well, do you think Dawkins and Co. would mind if I fine-tune their slogan and get a little more specific? Instead of "There's probably no God, so stop worrying and enjoy yourself", how about "There's probably no God, so stop worrying and get smashed". Is that okay?'

'I don't see why not,' he replied. 'It's your body. Do what you like with it.'

'Okay, let's try another couple: "There's probably no God, so stop worrying and go smash something up." Or how about, "There's probably no God, so stop worrying and go smash someone up—whatever takes your fancy, just make sure you don't get caught."'

'Oh, come on!' he cried. 'Don't be so absurd.'

'Steady on, Alex,' I replied, 'it almost sounds as if you are about to declare certain actions to be wrong. Could it be that you do believe in truth—albeit your own—after all? Let's try another: "There's probably no God, so stop worrying and go ahead and commit adultery, steal, lie, cheat, whatever."'

'This is ridiculous!' he said. 'There are limits.'

'Limits?' I said, feigning shock. 'But this is just awful. There I was thinking that, because we live in a universe that began by chance, where life started by a little bit of luck and where we really are just pieces of assembled dust with no God to judge us, no transcendent truth, no ultimate destiny and no ultimate purpose, I really could stop worrying and go and do whatever I wanted! I thought that that was what the ad was saying. So I decided I wanted to go and smash something up, just for a laugh—you know, enjoying myself, just like the ad promised I could— but now you tell me that I can't do this and that I'm still under some kind of restraint! Well, that's just too bad! If we really do live in the chance-by-luck-no-God-no-truth-no-ultimate-destiny-or-purpose-universe, then I understand perfectly why getting smashed is fine. But tell me, I'm just having a little difficulty understanding what is wrong with smashing things up or smashing people up or lying, stealing, cheating, committing adultery or whatever tickles your fancy?'

You know, it probably never occurred to the British Humanist Association or Professor Dawkins how much they opened themselves up to potential lawsuits arising from their advert. In these crazy times of litigation and political correctness, the following scenario is a distinct possibility: some guy goes out and smashes someone up or commits some other dreadful crime. He is caught and gets sentenced to some pathetically lenient jail term by a humanist judge who doesn't really believe in punishment for crime but nevertheless bleats on about the severity of the sentence he is handing down. But once inside jail, the guy uses human-rights legislation to successfully sue the BHA and Professor Dawkins on the grounds that he saw their ad and, because he really enjoys smashing people up or stealing or raping, believed that he could now go and do it without worrying.

Perhaps the BHA should have been a bit more specific about how far we can go in enjoying ourselves without worrying in a godless universe, or at least put a disclaimer at the bottom, something like, 'The BHA and Professor Dawkins accept no responsibility for the actions of people who suppose that the probable non-existence of God means they really can stop worrying and enjoy themselves in ways that we ourselves wouldn't necessarily approve.' But then, such a disclaimer might just have led people to see that having got rid of God, they were now attempting to take his place.

Alex's reply was predictable—there's a great difference between abusing your own body or things and someone else's.

'Yes, I know you know that,' I replied, 'but not everyone necessarily shares "your truth"! Some people clearly believe that it is okay to go around smashing things or people up. Who are you to say they are wrong when you say you don't even believe in truth?'

This is probably the greatest point of tension in the unbeliever's position. He wants to deny God, so he must also deny the existence of transcendent truth, implying that it's okay for everyone to have their own version of the truth.

But this neat little theoretical trick is smashed into practical smithereens as soon as someone comes along with their own version of the truth that the unbeliever disagrees with. At that point, he protests that such and such behaviour is wrong or evil, even though in denying the existence of truth he has effectively denied himself any basis he could have had for saying such a thing.

So how does atheism resolve this problem? There are only two methods. The first is to ignore it and to cherry-pick bits of Christian morality that you like while rejecting those that you don't. Needless to say, this is somewhat disingenuous, and it only really works while you live in a society that has some Christian principles.

The only other way is to try to find some way of imposing 'transcendent truth' on people using a human institution. Step forward the only contender: the state. The only problem is, the course of history tends to show that whenever and wherever this is attempted, the state generally does a mighty fine job of performing all the things Alex would presumably have protested about as being wrong. Like stealing excessive amounts of money from people as if it had an absolute right to it, which is done through the clever substitution of the word 'taxation' for 'theft'. Like lying and deceiving the people when it suits it. Like oppressing and coercing various groups of people who don't share its particular view of truth. But because it is seen as the ultimate authority in a godless universe, it is, by and large, allowed to get away with these things. As Benjamin Franklin warned us: 'Man will ultimately be governed by God or by tyrants.'[1]

For his part, Alex disagreed with all this, and for good measure said that it was 'a classic example of extremist Christian fundamentalism, loaded with simplistic black-and-white thinking'. At least I think that was how he put it! Actually, I found his description rather fetching and was rather glad of it because it brought me nicely on to the other great problem with adopting Pilate's 'What is truth?' maxim: beneath the mountain of platitudes adopted by the relativist, such as 'there are no right and wrong answers' and 'everybody's opinions are equally valid', people never really act in this way in their everyday lives. Rather, black-and-white thinking is ingrained in us—not just in the extremists like me, but even in the 'moderates' like Alex. I explained it to him like this:

The basic starting point of truth and logic is A equals A, so A cannot equal non-A. Up to the nineteenth century, people generally thought in these terms: thesis or truth (A equals A) stands opposed to its antithesis or falsehood (A equals non-A). Then along came philosophers such as Hegel and, a century later, Satre, who, even if people aren't aware of them, have had a massive influence on the way they think today because basically they tore up these rules. In layman's terms, Hegel essentially said that although A seems to equal A, it ain't necessarily so, and the answer may change over time. Sartre then came along later and essentially said that A equals whatever you want it to equal.

Of course, it sounds ridiculous when expressed in these basic terms, but nevertheless this type of thought has filtered down to the general public, so much so that many people—on the surface, that is—now think in relative, subjective terms rather than in absolute, objective terms, and think themselves to be jolly, free-thinking people because of it. So the most enlightened person today is one who says things like 'What is truth?' or 'How can we know what truth is?' or 'Maybe this is just a dream I'm having', whereas someone who says, 'No—truth is absolute and we can know it because God has revealed it to us' is a boneheaded fool.

But the trouble is that no matter how multicoloured (as opposed to black and white) and liberal people like to think their opinions are, they always betray in their lives that, deep down, they do essentially still think in terms of A equals A, because this is the way we are made to think. Even if you are a 'What is truth?' person or a 'Your truth is your truth, and my truth is mine' wannabe, you will still find that, if you analyse your thoughts and words truthfully (if I'm allowed to use that word), your thinking is essentially in black and white in every essential area of life. You believe that Adolf Hitler was a wicked man? Black-and-white thinking! You believe that someone who punches you in the face for no reason has done something wrong? Black-and-white thinking! You believe that $2 + 2 = 4$? Again, black-and-white thinking!

If you really want to avoid thinking in black and white, you must fulfil the following criteria:

- Never, ever judge anybody for anything they do, either accusing them or excusing them for their actions, even in your thoughts.
- Never use the words 'good' and 'bad' when describing either an object or an action.
- Never use the terms 'right' and 'wrong' about anything.
- Never use language that implies that a person's behaviour, words or thoughts are good or bad / right or wrong (like 'extremist' or 'fundamentalist', for example).
- In short, never hold any opinions about anything or make value judgements about anything or anyone, all of which are examples of black-and-white thinking.

If you can do all these things, you will not only be the first person in history who has managed to do it, you will also be the most enlightened, free-thinking being in the world. But a word of warning: if you ever come to congratulate yourself on your liberal, multicoloured thinking in contrast to the black-and-white thinking of certain fanatics, you ought to be careful. Even this very comparison betrays black-and-white thinking at its very root.

After I had relayed all this to Alex, he sat pondering what I had said for a moment and then changed the terms of the debate somewhat:

'Look, my point is not necessarily that there is no truth, it is rather "How on earth can we know what is the truth?" When I say that your thinking is black and white, I mean that you have this book that you claim to be the truth, and you arrogantly believe you have all the answers to Life, the Universe and Everything. Even though you cannot possibly verify it, you will still bring God into everything, ramming your religion down people's throats on every occasion.'

Objection 5

I had suspected this would come. The subtle myth of neutrality! It works something like this: Christians believe that God exists, right? Unbelievers, on the other hand, believe that God doesn't exist, right? And neither side can prove their claim, right?

Now let's imagine that a Christian and an unbeliever are having a discussion—let's say, about the increase in crime in Western countries. If the Christian wants to mention that the increase in lawlessness just happens to be occurring at the same time as the Christian faith is being abandoned in the West and that these two things are intrinsically connected, he is, of course, going to have to mention God. And it is at this point in the discussion that he may well be told to 'stop ramming your religion down my throat' or suchlike. By which the unbeliever means 'Hey, buddy, I thought we were having a discussion about crime, and suddenly you've stepped way over the line of neutrality and now you're trying to foist your religious beliefs on me.' But is it really the case that the unbeliever is adopting neutral territory?

For the unbeliever, even though his view of crime—why it exists, why it has increased in recent years, what its cure is—is intrinsically connected to his belief that there is no God, he doesn't actually ever have to mention 'non-God' in order not to bring God into the discussion. He just doesn't mention God. And so, while the Christian is busy mentioning God and the unbeliever is busy not mentioning 'non-God', the impression given is that the Christian is bent on foisting his religious beliefs on all and sundry, whereas the unbeliever is the epitome of perfect neutrality and would never dream of ramming any of his beliefs down anyone's throat. Except, of course, that he does it all the time, albeit in a way that is much harder to spot, because his core belief is a negative presupposition rather than a positive one.

And it is this very point of alleged neutrality that is being used to hack away at the foundations of Christian civilization, even as you read this. Just take a look at the culture wars that are taking place in most Western countries at present. The unbelievers who have controlled these countries for the past few decades have adopted some of the most radical programmes of social reform that the world has ever seen, all in an unbiblical direction and all entirely unneutral. But as soon as someone rises up to challenge what is going on and invokes the 'G'-word, the most militant unbelievers cry foul, throwing their hands into the air in uproar, screaming about keeping God out of politics, out of economics, out of the schools, out of the law, out of sexual ethics, out of the abortion clinics, out of anything and everything, except that maybe they'll let believers keep him for a few hours on a Sunday.

And this is the way that the secular humanists silence any real opposition to their agenda—by painting themselves and their agenda as completely neutral and therefore utterly harmless, so that anyone who invokes the 'G'-word to oppose them must be automatically barred from the debate. In this way, they are able to deny freedom of speech and of thought, successfully cover up their own underlying assumptions and get away with 'ramming their non-God beliefs and agenda down our throats' on a daily basis.

After I'd said all this, Alex asked what it all had to do with the discussion of the truth.

'The point is this,' I answered. 'You play the "What is truth?" card, not because you believe it deep down, but because it suits your purpose. Why? Firstly, because admitting absolute truth is as good as admitting the existence of God, which is of course unpalatable to you; and secondly, because it enables you to sound reasonable and tolerant in contrast to my fanaticism.

'But then you find that you can't actually live with this position, because although you might like to believe that two or more truths can coexist perfectly alongside each other, they only do so until another person does something that clashes with your own truth, and then suddenly you're not so tolerant. And indeed, everything you've said to me today has clearly demonstrated that you have your own version of the truth, that you think in black-and-white terms and that you are as fundamentalist as I am.

'So the only escape route left for you is to attempt to present your "truth" as being perfectly neutral, in contrast to a nut like me who is way off beam. But this is clearly not the case, which is why I have tried to show that the unbeliever's position is as partial, albeit in the opposite direction, as mine.'

'Partial it may be,' he replied, 'but way off beam? I don't think so. That coming from someone who presumably believes that dead people can come alive again is a bit rich, don't you think? Isn't that the very definition of irrational?'

Notes

1   http://en.wikiquote.org/wiki/Empire:_Total_War#Benjamin_Franklin.

Objection 6: Christianity is irrational

There are two invisible unicorns in the camp. They cannot be seen, heard, tasted, smelled or touched, they cannot escape from the camp and they eat nothing. The only proof of their existence is contained in an ancient book handed down over countless generations. Can you disprove their existence?

As Alex popped to the toilet and I thought on the subject of irrationality, I recalled the 'Invisible Unicorn Challenge', which was one of the main attractions at Camp Quest, an atheist summer camp for children in the UK that aims to be a 'godless alternative' to traditional 'religious' camps and that claims to be 'dedicated to improving the human condition through rational inquiry, critical and creative thinking, scientific method ...'[1]

In case you hadn't guessed, once the children have seen the irrationality of trying to disprove the existence of the unicorns, they are then meant to go away and live the rest of their lives thinking that God is a synonym for unicorns. It is, of course, just another version of Bertrand Russell's Teapot, but did you spot its total disdain for rational inquiry, critical and creative thinking and scientific method?

Let me ask you a question: Was Jesus real? Disregarding the 5 per cent who can never make their minds up in opinion polls and always say 'don't know', at this point you've really only got one of two options: you can either say 'yes' or say 'no'. Now, if you say 'no', the danger is that you make yourself look utterly irrational and foolish. For you are flying in the face of the entire testimony of the last two thousand years of history, which points overwhelmingly to the reality of Jesus. Which is why no more than a handful of unbelievers are prepared to come out and say, 'Jesus didn't exist.' They know they might as well deny the existence of

William the Conqueror, Elizabeth I and—when nobody is left alive to remember it—the Holocaust.

But if you say 'yes', the next question you have to answer is this: Why do you think he was real? You could point to many secondary reasons, such as 'My parents told me about him' or 'We learned about him in Sunday school' or 'The testimony of history for the last two thousand years seems to point overwhelmingly to his existence'. But whatever secondary reasons you have, they can all be traced back to a single primary reason, which is this: because it says so in the Bible! Perhaps you have never read the Bible, or you are an atheist, Muslim, Buddhist or whatever. No matter: if you answered 'yes' when asked whether Jesus was real, regardless of your beliefs, you did so because it says so in the Bible. In other words, you believe in the existence of somebody, the primary proof of which is contained in an ancient book handed down over countless generations!

All of which is, of course, entirely rational and should give you no cause to question your sanity. But this being the case, you then have to ask yourself the following question: If I am prepared to believe in the existence of a real Jesus primarily on the basis of an ancient book handed down over countless generations, which is the more rational action: to accept what that ancient book claims about him—his divinity, his miracles, his sinless life, his resurrection—or to reject it? On what grounds do I accept that book's veracity regarding Jesus' existence, but then reject its veracity regarding everything else?

Essentially you have three choices:

1. To reject everything that the ancient book handed down over countless generations says, even regarding the very existence of Jesus.
2. To accept what the ancient book handed down over countless generations says about Jesus' existence, but then reject what it says about him, what he did, what happened to him and who he was.
3. To accept everything that the ancient book handed down over

countless generations says, not only regarding Jesus' existence, but also what it says about him, what he did, what happened to him and who he was.

Only one of these options is strictly rational!

The Camp Quest game was therefore not just attacking the existence of God; it was undermining the entire nature of rational, scientific, historical enquiry. Which is why the not-so-smart kids would have come away from the camp thinking, 'Unicorns and God—they're all the same to me.' The slightly smarter kids would have come away thinking, 'Well, if it's irrational to believe in somebody or something that I can't see purely on the basis of ancient documents handed down through the generations, then my history teacher might just as well teach me about the tooth fairy alongside Julius Caesar.' But the really smart kids might just have asked the camp coordinator, 'Sir, do you believe Jesus was real?' and then quietly sniggered to themselves as the camp coordinator desperately attempted to squirm his way out of looking rather silly.

Alex had now returned, so we continued our discussion with me asking him what exactly he found so irrational about Christianity.

'Not sure that our journey is quite long enough for all that,' he replied. 'But I'll give you five things to chew on:

- That the universe was spoken into existence by a God who has always existed
- That the waters of the Red Sea were actually parted for long enough to allow thousands upon thousands of people to pass over
- That a virgin conceived a child
- That blind, deaf and lame people were instantly cured of their disabilities
- That a man rose from the dead and ascended up into heaven.'

'Okay,' I said nonchalantly, 'and what is it that you find irrational about these things?'

Alex's face contorted into a semi-disgusted, semi-pained expression, and he began to make weird spluttering sounds, all of which suggested that he perceived my response to be just about the most stupid answer I could have given. When he regained his composure, he said:

'What do I find irrational? Well, let's see! I have never actually seen flowing water standing up straight; never known a virgin to conceive; never heard of blind, deaf and lame people being healed by being touched or spoken to; and I have never seen a man rise from the dead, let alone fly off into the air. If I had seen any of these things or heard about them anywhere, then I would have no trouble in believing them. But as it is, I haven't—and nor have you—and so I would have thought that the word "irrational" was rather a good one, wouldn't you?'

I considered his statement for a few moments and then answered as follows:

'There are several interesting things in what you have said that I should like to pick up on. Firstly, all of the incidents you have just mentioned are stated in the Bible as either one-off episodes or at least confined to a specific period of time, and therefore it comes as no surprise that you have not seen or heard of any like occurrences. For example, when Isaiah prophesies of the virgin conception some seven hundred years before it actually happened, he says: "Therefore the Lord himself shall give you a sign; behold, a virgin shall conceive, and bear a son, and shall call his name Immanuel" (Isaiah 7:14).

'The fact that this event was described as a sign was precisely because it was a "once in the history of the world" episode. If one in every hundred virgins conceived, it wouldn't be much of a sign, would it? And so the failure of all other virgins before or since to conceive would seem to have precisely nothing whatsoever to say regarding the rationality or irrationality of the event.

'Secondly, you have fallen into the great logical error of assuming that unless you have personally had experience of something or heard of something, it cannot possibly be true. Well, I have no first-hand experience of your wife and your children, but it does not appear to me to be at all irrational to accept that they exist, given what you have told me.

'But the third interesting point, and by far the most important with regard to the rationality of these things, is that you failed to mention the first item on your original list. What was it now—"that the universe was spoken into existence by a God who has always existed". Tell me, why didn't you tell me that Christianity is irrational because you have never seen a universe spoken into existence?'

'It wasn't deliberate,' he said, shrugging his shoulders. 'I might just as easily have used this example as any of the others.'

'Not exactly,' I replied. 'The issue of the universe being spoken into existence may well fall into the category of something which you have not personally had experience of, but there is a crucial difference between this point and all the others you mentioned. With all the other objections you raised, it is possible—hypothetically, that is—that you could have been there, as all the events you mentioned were testified to by human witnesses. But with regard to the question of the universe being spoken into existence by a pre-existing God, this is not the case, as by definition no human was there to see it nor could have been.

'What this means is that although you may theoretically be able to judge the rationality of the other miracles you mentioned by whether you have ever seen or heard of them occurring, the simple fact is that you cannot possibly do this with the issue of the universe being spoken into existence by a God who has always existed. As God says to Job and his friends, "Where were you when I laid the foundation of the earth? Tell me, if you have understanding" (Job 38:4). And furthermore, because you cannot possibly do this, this in turn has crucial implications for your assertion that belief in the other miracles you have mentioned is irrational. Do you see what I am getting at?'

'Not really, I'm afraid.'

'What I am saying is this: ultimately, the rationality or irrationality of miracles does not depend one iota on whether such events occur today or not, as you have implied, but on just one simple question—is the universe the product of completely "naturalistic" causes or is it the product of an infinite-personal God? If it is the latter, the "problem of miracles" simply vanishes away. So I want to see if you agree with this very simple statement: If the universe was created by an infinite-personal being, then events such as the parting of the Red Sea and the incarnation, miracles, and the resurrection and ascension of Jesus Christ are no more inconceivable than you and I sitting here having this conversation.'

'I don't have a problem with that,' he replied, after giving it some thought, 'as long as you don't have a problem with this equally simple statement: If the universe was not created by an infinite-personal being, then events such as the parting of the Red Sea and the incarnation, miracles, and the resurrection and ascension of Jesus Christ are infinitely more inconceivable occurrences than you and I sitting here having this conversation.'

'On one level, yes,' I replied. 'If the universe is entirely naturalistic, then such miracles would seem to be absurd. But on another level, regardless of whether the naturalistic explanation of origins is even feasible, there is a glaring problem with your position.'

He beckoned me to continue, so I went on:

'It all hinges around the definition of the word "miracle". Let me ask you if you agree with this definition: a miracle is a contravention of the normal laws of nature normally attributed to supernatural intervention.'

After he had thought about this and then indicated his approval, I continued:

'Okay, the question of miracles encompasses two things: firstly, there is the normal state of physical, chemical and biological affairs; and secondly, there is the miracle itself, which is a deviation from this norm. Now, beginning with the great infinite-personal God, this presents no problem. By definition, in his universe he would have perfect freedom and power to alter these laws if he wished to do so.

'But for a naturalist such as yourself, the problem is not on the miracle side of things as such but on the normal state-of-affairs side. Your very reason for rejecting miracles is because they run contrary to some kind of unalterable natural law. But the irony of this is that your whole position rests on the denial of the very existence of a lawgiver who could give and sustain such an unalterable law. Instead, you maintain that the universe is somehow the product of blind and random forces. Which means that beginning from your basic position, it's not really miraculous deviations of normal natural laws that you should have a problem with—in a sense, they should occur all the time in a random universe—but rather the fact that there is any "normal" state of affairs in the first place from which to judge them from.'

'This is not exactly the case,' said Alex. 'You are right to say that miracles are, by definition, aberrations of the normal state of things, and you are also right to say that an infinite God would have no problem in bringing about these deviations, but your whole case breaks down not here but further back in the grand scheme of things—that is, with the existence of this infinite God, which you cannot prove.'

I had a strong sense of déjà vu at this point and imagined that we must have just pulled out of Waterloo Station a couple of minutes ago. But just as I was wondering whether to call it quits and ask what flavour of sausages his wife would be cooking that night, it occurred to me that his answers were pretty similar to those I would have given a few years ago, before my conversion. So despite my misgivings, which I'm sure he felt too, I continued:

'Let me just recap for a moment or two,' I said. 'You began by informing me that you perceive Christianity to be irrational because it asks you to believe in miracles. We have then gone on to at least agree that if the universe was created by an infinite-personal God, the "problem of miracles" disappears. So we have, somehow or other, come to the point where we can say that the existence or non-existence of miracles does not hinge on the feasibility or probability of the event itself; instead, it hinges purely on the question of whether God does or doesn't exist. Would you agree with all of that?'

'Yes, I think so,' replied Alex.

'And by extension, the question of whether Christianity is irrational does not hinge on whether virgins conceive or whether men can turn water into wine or whether the dead can come back to life. Rather it hinges solely on the question of whether the infinite-personal God exists. Are you happy with that?'

'Yes,' he said, 'so that if he doesn't exist, the problem of miracles remains for you, and Christianity is, as I say, irrational.'

'Agreed,' I replied, 'but without revisiting the whole existence question again, which I believe we've covered enough, at least we seem to have reached the point where we can say this: the "problem of miracles" is just a red-herring argument that has nothing whatsoever to say about the rationality or irrationality of Christianity. Instead, the reasonableness of Christianity rests solely on the existence or non-existence of God.'

'Not exactly solely,' he countered. 'Let's move on from the question of the plausibility of miracles. Maybe neither of us can prove the authenticity or falsehood of them, but what I can do is to point to aspects of Christianity occurring today which are utterly irrational.'

'Go on,' I encouraged him.

'Well, the obvious one that springs to mind is praying,' he replied. 'Let's say a Christian couple have a baby that becomes seriously ill. They will obviously both pray for it. Now, if the child recovers, they will tell me that "their prayers were answered", and they will expect me to accept this as proof of "God's hand" in it. But if it dies, will they turn round and say, "God didn't answer our prayers" or "Okay, we were wrong, there is no God"? No, they will just say, "God heard our prayers, but it was his will that our baby died." It's a no-lose situation. If the baby lives, God exists and is good; if the baby dies, God exists and is good. Is this what you call rational?'

'Well,' I replied, 'I would point out that as far as you are concerned, it is a no-win situation. If the baby lives, God doesn't exist; if the baby dies, God doesn't exist. Is this what you call rational? But let me give you another scenario. Let's say a non-Christian couple have a baby that becomes ill. They don't pray for it. They might "keep their fingers crossed" or just "hope" that it gets better, but they don't pray to the triune God of heaven and earth. Now, if the child recovers, they will tell me that the child was "very lucky"—as if its life had been preserved by some kind of cosmic lottery.

'But if the baby dies, what will they say? You will almost certainly get one of two reactions. In some cases there will be those who, without ever before or after showing any true belief in God, nevertheless start saying stuff about their child being in a "better place". In other cases, the death of the child will be seen as the final proof that there is no God, and even though they never acknowledged God as the giver of that child's life, let alone prayed to him to spare it, the parents will end up harbouring anger in their hearts at the God whom they claim doesn't exist. But the one reaction you can guarantee that you won't hear a couple saying is this: "Oh well, the child was just unlucky, but never mind—it was only cosmic dust in a random universe after all."

'So which is the more rational and logical position? It must surely be the one that is entirely consistent with itself, regardless of whether the baby lives or dies. You imply that the Christian couple are being inconsistent when they still believe in God even though their prayers apparently weren't answered. You think that therefore they are acting irrationally and illogically. But the fact is that they do act consistently throughout, because their basic assumptions do not once change. They believe that their baby was a gift from God before and after its death. They know that their baby was special because it was made in the image of God before and after its death. They know that the Bible tells them to pray in such circumstances, but they also know that it nowhere promises them that God will necessarily answer their prayers by sparing their child.

'In fact, there is an example of exactly this situation in the Bible, where King David prayed to God to spare his baby son, but the baby died nevertheless (2 Samuel 12:15–23). But the fact that this didn't turn David from continuing to trust in God—and the fact that the Christian couple continue to trust in God whatever the outcome—shows that their belief is entirely consistent throughout.

'By contrast, the unbelieving couple whose baby dies are entirely inconsistent throughout. By never attributing the child's life to God or asking him to preserve its life, they actively demonstrate their belief that they live in a random and impersonal universe. Yet at no point in either the baby's life or death do they ever act towards their child in the way you might expect them to if they really believed the child to be a randomly produced bunch of animate atoms. While the child is alive, they "hope" that it will survive. Hope in what? Hope it gets lucky in the cosmic lottery? Hope in nothing? Hope even in hope, whatever that is? And if the baby dies, do they follow through their own logic, shrugging their shoulders and saying, "Oh well, that's the purposeless universe for you"? Of course not. They either harbour some hope that their child has not been annihilated or they blame the God whose existence they deny for doing this to them, rather than pondering whether the outcome might have been different if they had prayed for the child in faith. Either way, their reaction is utterly inconsistent with their beliefs and therefore totally irrational. I could weep over it! If only they had faith and understood the ways of God, perhaps they would come to see that their baby's death was not for annihilation or for no purpose, but—as King David saw with regard to his son—maybe it's possible that God *out of his mercy* took that child from this present evil world of suffering and tears and gave it an everlasting abode in that place where there is "no more death, neither sorrow, nor crying, neither shall there be any more pain" (Revelation 21:4). That puts a rather different slant on the event, does it not?'

After several moments, Alex responded: 'You know, what strikes me about your arguments is that you seem to be denying that Christianity is actually a faith. You are trying to prove your position and are at pains to keep saying that it is perfectly rational. But the fact is, Christianity *is* a faith. Faith is the opposite of reason. Therefore Christianity is irrational.'

'Firstly,' I replied after some deliberation, 'I am not denying in the slightest that my position is a faith and that it requires the exercise of faith. The Bible is clear that it does, saying that "the just shall live by faith" (Romans 1:17) and that "without faith it is impossible to please [God]" (Hebrews 11:6).

'Secondly, I am not trying to "prove" my faith. You described Christianity as irrational, and I have simply been trying to show that it is not as barking mad as you seem to think, while at the same time trying to show you that your position is perhaps not quite as sound as you seem to think.

'What amuses me about your claim is that it suggests that those outside the Judaeo-Christian framework have solved all the riddles of life aeons ago, and ridiculous Christians like me are just clinging on to our silly old superstition in spite of the fact that the answers have been discovered, tested and proved. Whereas what has actually happened is that secular philosophers—from Plato to the latter eighteenth century—failed in their quest to find a rational, unified meaning to life, and since that time, philosophers have sought answers not in the rational, but in the non-rational. We've had the existentialists who said that life was simply absurd and that truth and meaning are entirely subjective; we've had the likes of Aldous Huxley who said that meaning to life could be found in perfectly healthy people taking drugs; and we've had the likes of Karl Jaspers who said that the answer lies in people having some kind of "final experience" which gives life some sort of meaning.

'But all these attempts have been—rather predictably—miserable failures, and we now find ourselves in a day when the only "philosophical" values by which most non-Christians in the West live their lives are a total apathy regarding the great questions of Life, the Universe and Everything and a desire to live a life of what the great theologian and philosopher Francis Schaeffer termed "personal peace and affluence".

'Now contrast this to Christianity, which was set in stone just under two thousand years ago. True, men have often perverted its meaning throughout that time and have had great disputes over some of its doctrines, yet the fundamental truths of true Christianity are exactly the same now as they were when they were first written down. Now, I realize that the longevity of Christianity does not on its own prove its rationality or truth, but to stand in the stream of all those secularists who have tried but clearly failed to find an answer to the basic questions of life and to lob the "irrational" insult over the wall at something that has stood the test of time—well, that is a bit rich, don't you think?

'And thirdly, I deny categorically that faith is the opposite of rationality, as you have said. I am aware that much of what passes for Christianity today is simply "religious existentialism", where truth is dependent on personal experience. But this is not biblical Christianity. Biblical Christianity is based on objective facts, and biblical faith is not the belief in spurious subjective stuff that we make up ourselves but the acceptance of the objective facts presented to us in the Bible. But by contrast, what objective facts can you point to in order to be acquitted of the charge that your faith is irrational?'

I had a feeling that he would ignore my question and set his guns on my assertion about the Bible. I was right about his ignoring the question, but, to my surprise, he took the conversation in a different direction:

'Objective facts? There is nothing objective or factual about it. It is just a fanciful delusion dreamed up by people who can't accept the real facts of life. That's what religion is! Just a crutch for people who can't face reality.'

Notes

1   http://www.campquest.org/mission.

Objection 7: Religion is just a crutch for people who can't face reality

O nce upon a time there lived a man who had a crutch. He was probably the most esteemed man on the planet at that time, one of the most powerful and, without doubt, the richest. This man commissioned great houses to be built for himself, as well as vineyards, gardens, orchards and woods to be planted. He lived in a palace and had many, many servants, thousands of animals, great possessions, and silver and gold by the truckload. He even had his own choirs and orchestras to perform for him at his whim. By his own reckoning, he was a materialist through and through, and any possession or material pleasure he desired he had to have, and he made sure he got.

But after he had amassed all this stuff, he did something one day that he had not done for a very long time. He thought! That's right, he actually thought! And do you know what he concluded? He looked at all the stuff he had amassed, all the possessions he possessed, all the pleasures he had experienced, and he realized that not one bit of it had brought him true happiness. It was nothing but vanity.

So he sold his crutch and bought another one. With the new crutch, he became the exact opposite of his former frivolous self, forgoing materialism for philosophy and becoming intensely serious for a while. Instead of collecting things and just looking for the next pleasure fix, he gave himself to learning. For a while things seemed to be okay, but then it gradually dawned on him that although his new ways were better than his former ways, he was still in exactly the same condition as before: as a hedonistic fool he was heading for death, and as a serious sage he was heading for the same place.

So he had tried hedonism, and it had made him sick. He had tried academia, and it had left him empty. And having done the rounds, he now felt utterly depressed. You might accuse him of simply not being able to face reality, but the fact is he had 'done reality' on a far more lavish scale than you or I could ever do. He had tasted the 'reality' of the unthinking life and the 'reality' of the thinking life, and at the end of it all, as he reached his old age, he could conclude nothing other than that neither of these 'realities' was actually the 'true reality'. If it was, he—along with every man, woman and child who had ever tried it—would have found true fulfilment in it instead of nausea and vanity. And so he had that strange but undeniably powerful feeling that has almost certainly entered the mind of every single human being who has ever lived at various times of their life: there must be more to life than this!

Thankfully, after he had seen the reality of the two crutches he'd made for himself, he didn't dampen his feelings as multitudes sadly do. Instead he answered the call from his Creator, turned to the ultimate reality, and finally found true meaning in both material things and ideas, and indeed Life, the Universe and Everything. Then he wrote a book to warn others not to follow in his folly. His name, by the way, was King Solomon.

'Tell me, Alex, when you accuse the "religious" of inventing a psychological crutch for themselves, it sounds suspiciously as if you are not including yourself and your fellow unbelievers in this category. May I ask why not?' I said.

'Because I'm an atheist,' he replied, looking at me as if I had lost the plot. 'We've been speaking to each other for about an hour now. Did you not pick that up from the conversation so far?'

'Oh yes,' I answered with a smile, 'but what I don't understand is why you think this excludes you from the charge of being religious.'

This time he no longer merely looked at me in a manner that suggested he thought I had lost the plot; he actually told me to my face that I had lost the plot. So I decided I had better attempt to explain myself.

I asked him if he took the view that a religious person is merely someone who believes in God. When he replied that he did, I asked him what he would say about pantheists who believe not in God as such but in some kind of life force which is in all of us and that we are all, in some mysterious way, God. He supposed that they too were religious. But what would he say about the man who believes that there is a tiny china teapot somewhere between Earth and Mars and that this teapot has magical powers that influence our lives and control our destinies? Would such a man be described as religious, even though he doesn't necessarily believe in God? Alex was happy to describe such a man as religious, and when I asked him why, given that the man doesn't believe in God, he responded by telling me that it was because he believes in something that he has not the slightest shred of evidence for and that is not even remotely credible.

'So, Alex,' I said, 'would you agree that you have now shifted your definition of religion from a mere belief in God to a belief in something for which a person cannot give a proper account?'

His reaction to my deconstruction of his position was to yawn nonchalantly and say 'And?' in such a way as to leave me in no doubt how little impression this had made on him. By no means discouraged, I carried on with a couple of more examples:

'What about the Egyptians who embalmed their dead because they believed in the afterlife? Were they committing a religious act, and if so, why?'

'Yes,' he replied. 'Why? Because they had absolutely no reason to believe that there was an afterlife, making it entirely a matter of faith.'

'Fair enough. But what about those who burn their dead for the opposite reason—because they don't believe in an afterlife? Are they committing a religious act, and if not, why not?'

'No, they're not,' he said. 'Why? Because there is no proof or evidence for an afterlife.'

'So what you are saying is that the absence of proof for life after death automatically confirms the opposite—no life after death—to be true,' I said. 'Not quite sure about this. If it's all the same to you, I would prefer it if you showed me your incontrovertible proof that we are annihilated at death.'

Objection 7

'I can take you to a grave and show you a stinking corpse, if you like,' he replied sarcastically.

'Not particularly,' I said. 'In any case, that wouldn't prove anything. We Christians are perfectly aware that bodies die and rot in the grave. Our bone of contention with you is not this point but that there is also something called the soul which leaves the body at death and which will be reunited with the resurrected body at the end of time. I am aware that I can't prove this, although I would say that there is overwhelming evidence for the existence of a non-material soul; but even so, it still takes a good deal of mental gymnastics to think that, because I can't prove life after death, this automatically proves your contrary assertion that the entire human being—including the soul—is totally annihilated at death.'

'Can you tell me where this conversation is leading?' he asked. 'We seem to have headed back to where we began—about proof and evidence. What's your point?'

'I'm just trying to establish a few things here,' I replied. 'Firstly, I'm trying to get a working definition of what religion is, so that I can answer your charge that religion is just a crutch for people who can't face reality. You started off by saying that religion was belief in God. Then you included things like pantheism in your definition. Then when I reintroduced Mr Teapot, who doesn't believe in God or the gods but only in a magical teapot, you were willing to proclaim him to be religious too. And finally, when I introduced the Egyptian practice of preparing the dead for the afterlife, you were quite clear that this was a religious act.

'Now I am in complete agreement with you on all these things. The Christian, the pantheist, Mr Teapot and the Egyptian—all are religious beings. But so too is the pagan who burns his dead. All of them are religious, not because they worship God or because they go to church, but simply because they have a fundamental set of underlying beliefs and assumptions—a worldview—that shapes the way they think, the way they speak and the way they live. As the proverb says, "For as he [man] thinketh in his heart, so is he" (Proverbs 23:7).

'So if I were to define religion, I would say it is any unprovable set of beliefs that addresses questions of our origins, purpose and destiny, the answers to which form a person's worldview and affect the way in which they live. Happy with this definition?'

After giving it a bit of thought, he nodded his agreement.

'Good,' I replied. 'And this brings me on to the second thing that I am trying to establish, which is that you might just find that you and your fellow unbelievers are not immune from the "disease" of religiousness yourselves. When you speak of "the religious", you speak as if you belonged to the only group of people in the world whose beliefs regarding the origins of life, the purpose of man and the ultimate destiny of man have been established as unquestionable facts. Ergo, anyone who doubts, questions or opposes these "facts" cannot be anything other than a madman with a crutch.

'But you know as well as I do that you can no more prove how we got here, why we are here and what happens to us after death than I can, much less provide any satisfactory answers to the great questions that face man. Yet you seek to hide this uncomfortable truth by using the words "religion" and "religious" to attack the apparent inadequacies of my position, purely so you can conveniently cloak the shortcomings of your own position. Your use of the word "religious" is not so much a distinction between those with the undisputed facts and those who rely on faith, but simply another way of saying "I'm right and you're wrong". Face it, Alex, you may not go to church or read a "holy" book or pray, but you have your own set of unprovable beliefs on the great questions of life as much as anybody else. And that, according to the definition we have both agreed on, makes you just as religious as me.

'And the last thing that I'm trying to establish is that if you do indeed hold to such a set of unprovable beliefs—that is, a religion—is it not just possible that *your* religion is just a crutch because *you* can't face reality?'

'Look,' he replied, 'I have no problem whatsoever with accepting reality. It is you and your ilk who are unable to accept that this life is all you're going to get, which is why you invent all sorts of spurious ideas about living for ever in heaven. Then you've got the nerve to accuse people like me of being "religious" on the grounds that I can't disprove the made-up fairyland you've invented in your heads.'

'Hold on, Alex,' I responded. 'I never claimed you were religious because you can't disprove my beliefs. I claimed it because you can't prove your own. Surely if your beliefs were as "unreligious" as you claim them to be, you would have no problem whatsoever in proving them?'

I think we both felt the conversation was getting a little heated, so I tried to move it past the question of what does and doesn't constitute religion to the question of reality, asking him what he thought about the following great realities of life:

- All people long for true, lasting happiness and a true purpose to their lives.
- Pain, suffering, disease and ultimately death mean that all are disappointed in their quest to achieve both true, lasting happiness and a true purpose to this life.
- Despite this horrible and obvious contradiction, for some reason multitudes never ask themselves why this might be, but instead continue to seek lasting happiness and purpose within a life that will inevitably disappoint them.

'Not true,' he replied. 'It is entirely possible to find happiness and purpose in this life. I am very happy and have lots of purposes, such as my marriage, my children and my job.'

'Well, as far as being happy is concerned,' I said, 'I don't doubt that you do indeed get pleasure out of your family, your hobbies and many other things, just as I do. But what I am talking about is something quite different. I am talking about true, perfect, lasting happiness. I'm talking about a happiness that cannot be diminished and that cannot be taken away. Now, I don't believe that you can say with any truth that your happiness is this type of happiness, because you are thwarted at every turn by events outside your control. For example, if you got home tonight and found out that your wife or one of your children had fallen ill, or worse, had died, would you still say you were perfectly happy? And you are also thwarted by events of your own making. Sorry to bring it up yet again, but I can't quite believe that arguing with your wife fits into the definition of perfect bliss.

'As for the question of purpose, again, all the things you have mentioned are good things that I would share with you. We were created to live happily in families, to work and to rest, but much as these things are all sound, they don't actually address the point I made. I was talking about people needing to find a purpose *for* their lives, but what you have given me is a list of purposes *within* your life. These are quite different things. I don't doubt that anyone, regardless of their beliefs, can find many purposes within their lives. They might be everyday purposes, such as going for a walk. Or they might be long-term purposes, such as careers and families. But when all is said and done, all of these things are purposes within our lives; none of them give us an ultimate purpose for our existence.

'So the reality of life is one awful contradiction: every one of us has an undeniable, unquenchable desire to find true happiness and true purpose, yet none of us are able to achieve this in this life, because circumstances foil us at every turn. This is the fundamental reality of human existence! Yet instead of admitting this glaringly obvious truth and seeking the answer to it, tragically the vast majority of people simply ignore it and continue to try to find true fulfilment and ultimate purpose for their existence in this life, even when reality screams to them that it cannot be done. So instead of being attuned to reality, as they like to make out, what they are actually doing is ignoring reality and turning away from it completely.'

Throughout history, people have set about concocting many different psychological crutches to prevent themselves from ever having to discover the answer to the paradox. Today, the main means in the Western world seem to be as follows:

The first is to ignore it completely. Apathy, sadly, gets the majority vote, and this can be achieved in a variety of ways, some of the most popular being TV, football, games consoles, drugs, celebrity worship, sex, alcohol, and so on. Don't misunderstand me: not all methods of ignoring thinking about meaning and purpose are wrong in and of themselves. Some of them are perfectly healthy and wholesome activities. It is just that when these things become our method of avoiding thinking about the meaning and purpose of life, they become futile and ultimately destructive.

The second means that has become very popular in recent decades is to turn all of life into a big joke. In *The Hitchhiker's Guide to the Galaxy*, for example, Douglas Adams gave the answer to Life, the Universe and Everything as forty-two. In *Monty Python's The Meaning of Life*, right at the end of the film, the answer to the meaning of life was presented as a sort of unimportant and incidental afterthought. Both were—deliberately —fairly pointless jokes. And this was their whole theme: life is a fairly pointless joke. Understand that this wasn't just comedy. It was a cultural expression of existentialist philosophy, which basically holds that there is no meaning to life and that life is absurd. So if it's absurd, why not laugh at it! Turn it into a joke! Of course, it's pretty easy to do this when you're young and things are going well; it's not so easy when someone you love dies or when you are in a nursing home living out your last few lonely years in pain and misery.

Then there is the third group. They go in completely the opposite direction to the jesters and take it all very, very seriously, deeply searching for some meaning to life. They may do this in many ways. Sometimes they choose to do so using some of the same methods as the first group— such as drugs or music—but unlike the first group, who do so in order to avoid thinking about Life, the Universe and Everything, this group does so because they hope to find some answers in these things. A lot of different answers are tried, but when they fail, sadly many such people end up in a desperate, even suicidal, state. If only they would stop ignoring the one answer they studiously avoid—that they are created in the image of an infinite-personal God, that they are rebels against him, but that he offers them free pardon if they truly repent and 'pleasures for evermore' (Psalm 16:11) if they seek their happiness and purpose in him. They would see that this really is the unified, coherent and satisfying answer to the meaning of life that they are seeking.

'Then, of course,' I went on, 'you have the much-maligned Christians who, for all their faults, do actually make a serious stab at finding out the meaning of life. And unlike the other three groups, they have an explanation that perfectly explains the contradiction between the desire to have purpose, meaning and happiness for our lives, and our inability to find it because pain, suffering, disease and ultimately death prevent us. The desire to have purpose is placed in us by God. Our rebellion against him is the reason this desire is frustrated, yet when we trust in his Son, he redeems us from this wretched, cursed paradox, and we really do find the happiness, meaning and purpose to our lives that we all yearn for. Yet of all these groups, it is the Christians who are labelled the ones with the crutch. But seriously, who is the man with the crutch—the one who truly seeks the answer to the meaning of life's paradox, or the one who drowns it out, laughs at it or seeks it in things that fail to answer it?'

'Or could it just be that I and the vast majority are able to live with the realities of life, while you obviously can't?' said Alex. 'I fully realize that bad things will happen, but I can live with it. I fully realize that I, my wife and my children will die one day, but I can still be happy in the here and now. But you are clearly unable to be happy knowing this about yourself and your family, which is why you choose to believe what you do about God, forgiveness, heaven and everlasting life. It is your crutch, without which you would have to face the simple reality—which would send you mad or into despair—that you're born, you live, you die.'

'As it happens,' I replied, 'I have no problem with the claim that you're born, you live, you die, since it is clearly true. We are born, we live and we will die. But if you mean it in the sense that you clearly mean it, I would reply that surely it must have crossed the mind of even the most thoughtless person who has used this phrase that it doesn't exactly explain a great deal. It doesn't explain how we got here. It doesn't explain what we should do while we are here. It doesn't explain why we get angry or upset with what other people do while they are here. It doesn't explain why we should bother trying to be nice to anyone else or if there is anything wrong with not being nice to others. It doesn't explain why we bother seeking a purpose while we are here, and it doesn't explain why people get upset when someone dies. In short, it explains precisely nothing—it is merely a slogan invented for the purpose of avoiding having to think about or explain the realities of Life, the Universe and Everything.

'As for you not having a problem with the fact that you or your family are going to die at some point, it doesn't surprise me in the least. You, and I assume your family, appear to be in the best of health, and I don't suppose that thoughts of death really enter your head very often. Even if they did, I'm quite sure that in your present healthy condition you would be utterly unable to empathize with or comprehend the true gravity of the situation in quite the same way as a man whose life is hanging by a thread.

'So if it's all the same to you, it may be best to wait until you're on an aeroplane at thirty thousand feet, when the pilot announces that the engines have failed and the plane is going down. When you realize that you're never going to see your wife and children any more, then perhaps it will be time to ask yourself whether or not you have a problem with dying. Or if your wife or your child is in hospital dying of cancer, perhaps then it will be time to ask yourself whether or not you have a problem with dying. In both scenarios, I think it unlikely that you will be heard uttering, "Oh well, you're born, you live, you die." But you might just find that in seeing your frailty and helplessness for the first time, maybe—just maybe—you will turn to the God who can save.'

'Aha!' he cried. 'Doesn't that just prove the whole point I'm making about religion being a crutch for the weak? Why is it always the outcasts and people who are "down on their luck" who turn to God? It's a dead giveaway. They've lost all hope, and so they have to find some from somewhere. And so they reach for the great lie in the sky, and suddenly life somehow doesn't seem quite so bad! As long as they continue believing, they can cope with life. It's not true what they believe—no doubt they know it deep down—but I suppose that if believing it makes them happy, then good luck to them! They now have their crutch!'

'You're right that it is a dead giveaway, but not exactly in the way that you have described,' I replied. 'Ask yourself this question: Why is it that the rich and powerful do not, as a general rule, become Christians? Why is it that when a man gains a fortune, he does not stop to thank God? Could it just be that when things are going well for us, and our pride is going full pelt, that the last thing we are ever going to do is to turn to God and thank him for prospering us? That would take humility, and humility rarely goes hand in glove with riches, greatness and power. You can just see Napoleon, at the height of his imperial power, humbly acknowledging God, can't you? No, but chain him alone to a rock on St Helena after his empire crumbles, and then listen to the change in him.'

Once again I used Alex's mobile to look up the quote: '"Now that I am at St Helena, alone, chained upon this rock, who fights and wins empires for me? What an abyss between my deep misery and the eternal reign of Christ, which is proclaimed, loved, adored, and which is extending over all the earth!"[1] You claim that men only turn to God when they are down and out. Very true! But rather than it being weak men inventing a crutch, could it just be that God has to humble us in our intolerable pride before we are prepared to admit our own weakness, our own sins and our own mortality?

'As for such people believing a lie yet knowing the truth deep down, that's an interesting observation, because that's just what the Bible says about people like you, Alex: they "changed the truth of God into a lie" (Romans 1:25). Why? Because "they did not like to retain God in their knowledge" (Romans 1:28). And why is that? Because admitting the existence of the God of the Bible means that your life begins to unravel. For the first time in your life you have to face the fact that you have lived a lie; you have to face the fact that you are not as good and as kind as you thought you were; you have to face the fact that you never really knew yourself before; you have to face the fact that the world does not revolve around you; and most alarmingly of all, you have to face the fact that you will be judged for breaking the laws of the infinite God.

'All this is very, very difficult to take. Far easier to just ignore these things and pretend that God doesn't exist, or if he does exist, that he will look very kindly on you and won't mind too much about you breaking his perfect and eternal laws. So you take up your crutch of unbelief, and this no doubt gives a great deal of comfort. I know what it's like because I used such a crutch to get around for many years. With it you can walk around happily pretending that no judgement awaits, and you can do pretty much what you like without fear of repercussions. But then you read the Bible, and the Spirit of God comes and kicks that crutch out from underneath you. As you fall to the ground upon that crutch and see it splinter into pieces, you suddenly see it for what it is and what it always was: just a crutch that you used to stop yourself having to come face to face with reality! Far easier and far more convenient to carry on with your crutch, ignoring reality and dismissing those who believe the Bible as weak, cranky losers.'

'The Bible?' replied Alex scornfully. 'Come on, nobody believes the Bible any more.'

Notes

1   J. S. C. Abbott, 'Napoleon Bonaparte', *Harper's New Monthly Magazine*, 10/56 (1855), p. 180.

Objection 8: Nobody believes the Bible any more

id you know that Hitler was democratically elected? He didn't come to power through a revolution or a putsch; he came to power because he got more votes than his nearest rival. This fact alone ought to dispel the modern myth that somehow democracy or the will of the people is always going to be good and right. If it's possible for one person to be wrong or mistaken or even for some people to be wrong or mistaken, then it must also be possible for most people to be wrong or mistaken.

All of which means that the fact that most people believe something to be true does not automatically mean that the thing *is* true. And likewise, the fact that most people believe something to be false does not automatically mean that the thing *is* false. Truth and falsehood exist entirely independently, outside opinions, and mass opinion cannot change a truth into a falsehood or vice versa any more than it can stop the sun from shining.

Now, I am not using this point to argue that the fact most people no longer believe the Bible means that it must be true. All I am saying is that the fact most people no longer believe the Bible to be true does not automatically mean that the Bible must be false. Rather, we must—as the old saying goes—judge the book by its contents and decide for ourselves whether the majority have got it right or wrong. There are still a few of us around who have done this—that is, read the whole book, rather than accepting that the majority must have it right—and have concluded that it is indeed true. And I cannot urge you strongly enough to at least give it a go yourself. Blindly accepting what the majority says today, what the schools say today, what the media says today, what your family says today, what I say today or what anyone else says today without checking it out thoroughly for yourself is nothing but a form of self-imposed tyranny. You are letting others do the thinking for you and decide truth and falsehood on your behalf. Don't stand for it any longer. Rise up, shake off the dictatorship of the majority and go and read the Bible for yourself. If you read it and still remain an unbeliever, then at least you can say that your conclusions are your own and not those foisted on you by others, most of whom have probably never even read it themselves in any case.

Back on the train, I began by asking Alex why he thought it was the case that nobody—except me and a few others—believes the Bible any more.

'Why would anyone believe it?' he retorted. 'It's clearly just a hotchpotch of writings by men who never even met each other.'

'In one sense I agree entirely,' I replied. 'It is a hotchpotch of different writings, and these were indeed written by a mishmash of different men—from kings to shepherds, from fishermen to tax collectors.'

'But even so, you are happy to use the book as the basis for life and truth?'

'Yes, I'm happy to,' I replied with a smile. 'There is no conflict between its having been written and assembled by men and its having a divine origin and direction. This is just what the Bible claims about itself: "For no prophecy was ever produced by the will of man, but men spoke from God as they were carried along by the Holy Spirit" (2 Peter 1:21).'

'And that's good enough for you, is it?'

'By itself, no,' I countered. 'But it isn't by itself, and the rest of the book gives me every reason to believe that it was written under divine inspiration.'

'Like what?' he said scornfully. 'Okay, why don't you give me, say, three reasons why I should believe that it came from God.'

I toyed with the idea of asking him for three reasons why I shouldn't believe it came from God but decided against it, on the grounds of it being rather too facetious. So off the top of my head, I gave him the following:

'Right, in no particular order: Firstly, although it was written by men, it just isn't at all what we would have expected, had it been constructed by men alone acting without divine inspiration. Judging by how men usually set out their decrees, we would probably have expected it to be one long list of bureaucratic rules and regulations about what we can and can't do. At first glance, there does seem to be a good number of laws in the Bible, but when you compare it with the reams of legislation on national and international statute books, the number is miniscule. Have you any idea how many laws, directives and statutes the European Union has in its books, for example? If you put them all together, it would make the Bible look like a wee little pamphlet.

'But even aside from this, if it had come from men alone, I would maybe have expected some philosophy in it and maybe a sprinkling of utopian political theory, but what do we actually get? Family histories, national and international history, stories, anthropology, poetry, proverbs and sayings, theology, laments, philosophy, songs of joy, songs of mourning, songs of love, songs of anguish, songs of victory, songs of affliction, songs of praise, songs of war, doctrine and practice, prophecies, the Gospel narratives and letters. The works of men alone? I think not!

'Secondly, much of the book actively denounces the very people who claimed the book as their own. I defy you to read through prophecies like Jeremiah's, Hosea's and Amos's and tell me that they were written by men acting alone. Why? Because most of the denunciations within these prophecies are directed towards "God's chosen people". How is this possible? Why on earth is a hugely significant portion of the Bible, which was transcribed by the Jews and held up as the Jews' own book, given over to denouncing their own wickedness and furthermore to showing their refusal to admit and repent of their sinfulness?

'Thirdly, it is more accurate in its description of humans than anything else ever written. If I had to point to one verse in the whole Bible that more than any other convinces me of the truth of it, it would be this.'

I opened my Bible at the epistle to the Romans. 'Here we are: "For when Gentiles, who do not have the law, by nature do what the law requires, they are a law to themselves, even though they do not have the law. They show that the work of the law is written on their hearts, while their conscience also bears witness, and their conflicting thoughts accuse or even excuse them" (Romans 2:14–15).

'Now, Alex, here's a little game you can play, perhaps in your office or back in your home. Listen out for each time your children or your wife or your work colleagues—or better still yourself—condemn others for their words or actions, and then ask yourself whether you've ever seen or heard those same people committing the same sin that they are denouncing in others. We do it all the time. Sometimes we excuse behaviour, perhaps our own or that of a friend or some celebrity we like, but then we go and condemn that same behaviour in others whom we don't particularly like. But whether we accuse or excuse, all we are really doing is declaring exactly what the Bible says about us: that we have the law written in our very being and that we use this to condemn or exonerate both ourselves and others, depending on what suits us.

'And for good measure, let me give you a fourth reason. The Bible may be a hotchpotch in terms of who wrote it, when it was written and the different literary styles contained within it, but yet it has a unity of theme, purpose and prophecy throughout the entire book. The grand theme of the whole book is of God's redemption, in a real space–time situation, of sinful, rebellious people. And where is this theme to be found? Perhaps I should ask where it isn't to be found. I can't think of any of the entire sixty-six books of the Bible that don't have this theme stated in some form or other. This utterly refutes the claim that it was written by men acting without divine direction, and this fact alone would convince me that it is something I ought to take seriously.'

'And what about all the contradictions it contains?' questioned Alex.

'What sort of thing are you referring to?' I asked him.

'How about this: the Old Testament view of crime and punishment was that we are to take an eye for an eye and a tooth for a tooth. But what does the New Testament say? In the Sermon on the Mount, Jesus actually says that we are not to take an eye for an eye and a tooth for a tooth but we are to turn the other cheek. Well, you're going to have to throw out either the Old or the New, but you can't keep both, that's for sure.'

'Well, if the directives you mentioned were addressed to the same category of people, I suppose you might be right. But they're not,' I replied. 'The first, which is in Exodus—maybe chapter 20-something—is not directed towards individuals, but towards the civil magistrate. In other words, the command sanctions public justice, not private revenge. But man being what he is, rather than understanding that the act of justice is to be carried out by the state, used this instead as an excuse for desiring his own private revenge. And it is this false notion that Jesus was correcting when speaking to his disciples. He is not saying that the civil directive for justice no longer applies. He is not saying that his disciples should not defend themselves. What he is saying is that his disciples ought to have a spirit which doesn't desire personal revenge but rather leaves vengeance up to the higher powers—the state and ultimately God—and that they ought to have a spirit which is willing to show mercy and forgiveness, even to their enemies.'

This seemed to throw him a little, as if it had never occurred to him that these two 'contradictions' could ever be reconciled. We spent a few minutes discussing some other apparent contradictions, such as the 'discrepancies' between the Gospel narratives, which generally can be explained by one of the following:

Just as we might tell the same piece of news or story or joke to different sets of people in different locations and just as we rarely, if ever, tell the same thing using exactly the same words, Jesus may just possibly have said the same thing on more than one occasion and may just possibly have used slightly different words each time. It's just possible, isn't it?

The Bible says that its writers were moved by the Spirit of God as to what they should write; they were not dictated to. That means they had a fair amount of scope to include what they wanted to include and to exclude what they wanted to exclude, not to mention regarding how they presented it. Go and read four newspaper articles covering the same event. It is highly unlikely that their reports will be exactly the same, word for word, and yet it is entirely plausible that all four reports are free from falsehood.

I'd like to be able to say that these considerations made Alex sit up with wide eyes and say, 'Oh yeah! You know, I've really never thought of it like that before', but in reality he just yawned and then moved the conversation on to what I call Dan Brown syndrome. This is a condition exhibited by people who have never read the Bible but have read *The Da Vinci Code*, which they feel qualifies them to pronounce the Bible as a sinister plot put together in the time of the Emperor Constantine for the purpose of subjugating the whole of mankind.

'Look,' said Alex, 'everyone knows that the Bible was cobbled together in some shadowy council three hundred-odd years after Jesus was supposed to have died.'

'Hold on a minute, Alex,' I replied. 'Are you suggesting that the Bible is the product of some kind of conspiracy?'

'If that's what you want to call it,' he replied.

'So let me get this straight,' I said. 'A moment or two ago, you were calling the Bible a hotchpotch of writings by men who never knew each other, which kind of suggests that the literature involved was diverse, to say the least. But now you are telling me, unless I'm very much mistaken, that when the canon of Scripture was agreed upon, it was done so by people whose aims were to brainwash people. Is that about right?'

'In a nutshell,' he retorted.

'But you must see that it can't be both.'

'I do not see that,' he replied. 'Why should I see that?'

'Well, on the one hand, you're charging the Bible with the heinous crime of being written by a group of very different people over a very long period of time, but now you're charging it with being effectively "published" by another group of men who were somehow able to take this bunch of totally different literature written in very different styles and cobble it together in order to control the masses by asserting that it was divine in origin.'

Once again, Alex looked distinctly unimpressed, so I put it to him that he should try the same experiment with other forms and periods of literature to see if it could be done. Choose a period of history, say the

Greeks and the Romans. Take a large dollop of Plato and Aristotle, add some Homer and Virgil, stir in Julius Caesar's *Gallic Wars*, mix it together with some Seneca and Cicero, and finally season with the letters of Pliny. When you've mixed it all together into one book, go out and sell it to men as a revelation from God, replete with complete unity of purpose and message.

Or if the ancients don't appeal, try a more modern recipe. Take the 'prophetical' writings of Orwell and Huxley, chuck in some songs by maybe Bob Dylan and John Lennon, put it in the blender with a bit of Dylan Thomas, stir in a speech or two by Dr Martin Luther King Jr. and then add a pinch of something bitter, like a bit of Solzhenitsyn. Again, try to sell it as a book with a single theme written under divine inspiration. You can't do it, because there is no unity there. But somehow the Bible does exactly this: it takes the writings of a hotchpotch of different men, living over a 1,500-year period and writing in a range of literary genres and styles, and still manages to come up with a book which has a unity of theme throughout.

'But I reckon there's an even more basic problem with your conspiracy theory,' I continued. 'Tell me, Alex, the writers of the Scriptures and the men who met to agree the canon—who were they attempting to brainwash?'

'Anyone gullible enough to swallow it,' he replied.

'Okay, so can you tell me what was in it for those you are talking about? I mean, when Moses wrote the Pentateuch or when Solomon wrote the Proverbs, were they thinking to themselves, "Ha! This'll force those gullible fools several millennia down the line into subservience"? If so, why? What was in it for them? And what about those who met to agree on the canon? Have you ever read the book of Ruth? What on earth is a book about a woman returning from abroad with her mother-in-law and eventually getting married doing in a book compiled together by fourth-century propagandists? And what did they think they were playing at when they included the Song of Solomon, a book condemned by many Jews and later the Victorian moralists as impure and dirty? If there's brainwashing there, I'm not entirely sure how it is done, why it is done and what exactly its goal is. But then again, I suppose if I've been properly brainwashed by it, I wouldn't know, would I? So perhaps you can tell me.'

'The purpose is to make us all good little citizens who do exactly what we're told without ever questioning anything. Just like Marx said—the opium of the masses.'

When he said this I'm afraid I just couldn't stop myself from bursting out laughing. Somewhat taken aback, Alex asked what exactly it was that was causing me so much mirth. So I replied that here I was, living in a world that is currently adopting practically every doctrine of Marxism and Cultural Marxism without even knowing it, where the state is virtually worshipped by millions, and here he was using Marx's charge of brainwashing and oppression against Christianity.

He asked me what on earth I meant, so I gave him just a few examples: Whom do we look to for the education of our children? The state. Whom do we look to for healing when we are sick? The state. Whom do we look to for provision in our old age? The state. Whom do we look to for 'advice' on what is and what isn't healthy? The state. Who comes up with miles and miles of regulations to make sure we are safe and happy? The state. Who deliberately destroys the family and then takes it upon itself to become a surrogate father to the millions of fatherless children it creates? All this and more, in direct accordance with the ideology espoused by the man who claimed that Christianity was a tool used by those in power for brainwashing and oppressing the people.

But what, I asked Alex, is the Bible's ideology on these subjects? Well, for one, it restricts the power of the state to just two things: punishing evildoers within the nation's borders and protecting the nation from evildoers outside its borders. Unless you fall into either class of evildoers, according to the biblical model, you are a free man who will never even come into contact with the state.

The contrast between the biblical ideal and modern, atheistic, power-hungry statism could hardly be more stark. For example, 1 Samuel 8 makes it pretty clear that any government that forcibly takes more than one-tenth of a population's wealth in taxation is exercising tyranny over them. What does that say about the current governments of the world, most of whom take half of the average person's wages through a multitude of different taxes? And more to the point, which society is the real tyranny doing the real brainwashing: the biblical ideal of the small state, which exists only to keep the peace and allow people to go about their lawful business, or our atheistic, big-state society which eats our money, destroys families and then has the affront to tell us how we ought to live?

He didn't answer this question directly, but, with some justification, came at it from the angle of attacking the church for its many past failings.

'Oh, and what about the church? Are you denying that the church has done the same thing that you are accusing the state of throughout history? What about fleecing the poor back in medieval times by threatening curses and excommunications if they didn't cough up? Are you denying that that sort of thing went on? Are you denying that the church and its hierarchy have gorged themselves and lived in luxury, while the poor lived all around them and they did nothing to ease their condition?'

'I have no wish to deny it,' I retorted. 'In fact, I'm happy to acknowledge it, because the one thing that connects it to what I said about the state is the fact that the Bible unequivocally condemns both. The point is not whether oppressors and tyrants have occupied positions of power within the visible church but rather what the Bible actually says about such men. Does it condone or condemn them? Your point backfires spectacularly on you, Alex, because the Scriptures categorically condemn such behaviour—regardless of whether they are done in the state or in the church—in some of the most stark warnings given throughout the entire book. Allow me to give you a few verses to prove what I mean.'

Once again I leafed through my Bible and came to a few verses that I could recall off the top of my head. They were:

Objection 8

He [God] shall judge the poor of the people, he shall save the children of the needy, and shall break in pieces the oppressor (Psalm 72:4).

Rob not the poor, because he is poor: neither oppress the afflicted in the gate: for the LORD will plead their cause, and spoil the soul of those that spoiled them (Proverbs 22:22–23).

Woe unto you, scribes and Pharisees, hypocrites! for ye devour widows' houses, and for a pretence make long prayer: therefore ye shall receive the greater damnation (Matthew 23:14).

At the end of this, I looked him straight in the eye and said, 'Now seriously, Alex, never mind what the "church" or "churchmen" have said or done. This is what the Bible says. You can point the finger at certain people or sections of the church at certain periods in history and use this as a tool to criticize the Bible if you want. But the truth is that the Bible not only predicts that wicked people will sometimes occupy high positions in the visible church, as with the state, but it also shows that their condemnation for doing so will be truly awful. Go read about Judas Iscariot, or read 2 Peter 2 or most of the prophets if you don't believe me.

'But besides all this, there is one more point that I ought to make against the charge that the Bible is somehow a book put together in some shadowy council for the purpose of subjugating people, and it is this: conspiracies tend to be dangerous and harmful to others. But what about the "Bible conspiracy"? Well, the Scriptures tell me to "love [my] enemies, bless them that curse [me], do good to them that hate [me], and pray for them which despitefully use [me], and persecute [me]" (Matthew 5:44). They tell me to "owe no man any thing, but to love one another: for he that loveth another hath fulfilled the law" (Romans 13:8). They tell me that "the fruit of the Spirit is love, joy, peace, longsuffering, gentleness, goodness, faith, meekness, temperance: against such there is no law" (Galatians 5:22–23). They say that "pure religion and undefiled before God and the Father is this, To visit the fatherless and widows in their affliction, and to keep himself unspotted from the world" (James 1:27).

They tell me to "honour all men" and to "love the brotherhood" (1 Peter 2:17). Now tell me, Alex, in all honesty, does this strike you as one of the world's more sinister, dangerous and wicked conspiracies?'

'Actually, I'm glad that you've brought these things up,' said Alex. 'Sure, you can bang on about loving thy neighbour and doing good as much as you like, but you really are on a hiding to nothing on this one. If Christianity were true, mightn't we unbelievers be able to see a little more evidence of the "fruit of the spirit" you talk about? I would have thought so, but as I don't, I can only come to one conclusion: it is a fraud. Christianity has failed to fulfil its promises.'

Objection 9: Christianity has failed to fulfil its promises

Alex and I had now been travelling companions for nearly an hour and a half, and after the heaviness of our conversation so far, we both thought that now would be a nice time to have a little break from it for a minute or so. We talked a little bit about our families and where we had met our wives, and then somehow the conversation took a detour and we ended up swapping our favourite jokes. This was Alex's: Two muffins are in the oven and one says to the other, 'Man, it's hot in here'—upon which the other muffin yells, 'Help! A talking muffin!!!'

For my part, I told him mine. Two men were walking through a desert and had all but lost hope of finding any water. In their desperation, they both saw a mirage in the distance. As they came closer to it, they realized it was some sort of market place, lined with stalls. So they came to the first stall and asked for water, but all the man had to offer was bowls of sponge, jelly and custard. So they moved on to the second stall and encountered exactly the same thing there. On through the market place they went, but on each occasion the same thing happened—they asked for water but were offered a bowl of sponge, jelly and custard. As they came away from the market, one of the men said to the other, 'That was very strange, don't you think?' The other man turned to him and said, 'Yes, that was a trifle bazaar.'

And with that, we returned once again to our discussion.

'Okay, Alex,' I said, 'Christianity has failed to fulfil its promises. So which promises are you looking at?'

'Well, let's see,' said Alex. 'It's now about two thousand years since Jesus supposedly ascended into heaven and the apostles began to preach the gospel, and here we are all these years later, and what do we find? The world is full of wars, murders, rapes, thefts, corporate greed and all sorts of evil things going on. Let's face it, it doesn't look like Christianity has really done the business, does it? It's had a fair crack of the whip, but I don't know—maybe time to ditch it for something that actually works?'

'If we're going to give Christianity a fair crack of the whip, I think we need to do two things,' I replied. 'First off, we need to be clear what the Bible does promise and what it doesn't promise. Then when we have found something that the Bible does promise, we need to look at whether it can or can't be verified by us on earth. Only then can we see whether the Bible fulfils its promises or not.

'Now, with regard to what the Bible does and doesn't promise, you've mentioned the prevalence of wars, as if wars were something which wouldn't occur if Christianity were true. But does the Bible actually ever promise this?'

At this point, Alex interjected with a verse from the Bible that showed him to be a little more clued up than I had perhaps given him credit for:

'Hang on a minute. I'm sure there's a prophecy where it says something about nations learning war no more and destroying their weapons.'

I told him that the passage he was referring to was from the prophecy of Micah, and after searching for it, I read it out in full:

But in the last days it shall come to pass, that the mountain of the house of the LORD shall be established in the top of the mountains, and it shall be exalted above the hills; and people shall flow unto it. And many nations shall come, and say, Come, and let us go up to the mountain of the LORD, and to the house of the God of Jacob; and he will teach us of his ways, and we will walk in his paths: for the law shall go forth of Zion, and the word of the LORD from Jerusalem. And he shall judge among many people, and rebuke strong nations afar off; and they shall beat their swords into plowshares, and their spears into pruninghooks: nation shall not lift up a sword against nation, neither shall they learn war any more (Micah 4:1–3).

'Well, there you go,' responded Alex. 'That seems pretty clear to me.'

'It does indeed,' I said. 'But the question is, when does this prophecy find its fulfilment? Some apply it in a spiritual sense to the whole of the period since Christ's apostles began to build the church. And they would say that the language symbolizes how the gospel will conquer individuals and nations and will bring peace wherever it is accepted.

'Now, I don't doubt that there is some truth in this explanation, and I don't doubt that the gospel has done just this wherever it has been received. But personally, I think that it will have a literal fulfilment at some point in the future when the whole earth will be submitted to the rule of Christ and there will indeed be a period when wars will cease. And if you accept this view, among all the other things that could be said about it, it clearly shows that until this period of history, the opposite will be true: the nations will not dispense with their weaponry, and they will not learn the way of peace.'

'Not if religion is still around,' remarked Alex sardonically, 'since it is the cause of all wars, as you know.'

'Well, apart from the Iraq war, the Falklands War, the Vietnam War, the Korean War, the Second World War, the First World War, the American Civil War, the Napoleonic Wars and hundreds of other conflicts throughout the history of the world, I suppose you might be right,' I replied with equal irony. 'But even aside from the fact that this is demonstrably untrue, I do wonder why unbelievers always pick on war to make their point about "religion", as if war were the only evil that ever existed. Are there no other evils in the world you can pick on to make your claim? Is Christianity the cause of all adultery? Is Christianity the cause of all divorce? Is it the cause of all child abuse? Is it the cause of all thefts? Is it the cause of all corporate greed? Is it the cause of little children squabbling with one another? Is it the cause of road rage? Is it the cause of all the nasty, hurtful comments that people make about each other behind their backs? Are the prisons full of murderers and rapists who killed and raped because of their love for Christ? I think you know the answer to that, Alex, and I'd say the one thing all these things have in common is not "religion" but rebellion against God. You might be on to something if you replaced the word "religion" with the word "sin" —as in "sin is the cause of all wars".'

'Look,' said Alex, ignoring my point completely, 'you claim that

Christianity hasn't failed to fulfil its promises, and yet it has clearly failed according to one of its most fundamental tenets: love thy neighbour as thyself. Tell me, where exactly has this ever been seen?'

'You're right that it is indeed a central tenet of the faith. But again, I can nowhere find that the Bible actually promises that people will fulfil this perfectly before the future eternal kingdom. There are countless examples of places, tribes and nations where the gospel has penetrated and the effects have been dramatic. But by and large, the Bible actually paints a picture of the general state of the world as being quite the opposite to the "love thy neighbour" ideal to which it calls men to live. For example, this is what the apostle Paul says in his epistle to the Romans:

And even as they did not like to retain God in their knowledge, God gave them over to a reprobate mind, to do those things which are not convenient; being filled with all unrighteousness, fornication, wickedness, covetousness, maliciousness; full of envy, murder, debate, deceit, malignity; whisperers, backbiters, haters of God, despiteful, proud, boasters, inventors of evil things, disobedient to parents, without understanding, covenantbreakers, without natural affection, implacable, unmerciful (Romans 1:28–31).

'So whereas you falsely assume that because wars and hatred are prevalent on the earth this somehow shows the failure of Christianity, I could just as easily claim that by pointing these things out, you have actually proved the truth of Christianity, albeit unwittingly, because these things fulfil predictions given in the Bible.'

I then moved on to my second point, which was about the verification of promises that the Bible does give:

'With regard to verification, biblical promises fall into three categories. Firstly, there are promises that can't be verified by any of us here and now because they refer to future events. For instance, the Bible promises that if a person puts their trust solely in the atonement made by Jesus Christ for sinners, God will raise that person up at the last day: "And God raised the Lord and will also raise us up by his power" (1 Corinthians 6:14).

'Secondly, there are promises that can only be verified by Christians. For example, "If we confess our sins, he is faithful and just to forgive us our sins, and to cleanse us from all unrighteousness" (1 John 1:9). And then there is a third category, which has to do with consequences that arise here on earth and therefore can be verified by both believers and unbelievers.'

I was just going to elaborate on this last point when Alex stopped me and picked me up on my second point:

'Hold on a minute. You said that only Christians could verify the promise that Christ will forgive their sins and cleanse them from all unrighteousness. But even leaving aside the question of whether they are really able to verify the forgiveness part or whether it's a delusion brought on as a result of wishful thinking, what about the claim of being cleansed from all unrighteousness? This is something I am able to verify, because I can see how Christians behave. And my conclusion? Christians do bad things and are generally no different from anyone else. And what can you say to that?'

This is not an uncommon tactic, implying that Christianity doesn't work or fulfil its promises because Christians do bad things. But, as I pointed out to Alex, here are just some of the things that are wrong with the charge.

First off, when Christianity promises that its true adherents will be cleansed from their sins, it makes it clear that this is a process that will take place over the course of their lives and not in an instant. Forgiveness of sins, says the Bible, takes place when someone becomes a Christian. But the cleansing from sins only begins at this point. This being the case, it is obvious that throughout their lives, believers will still be doing many wrong things. So coming along and saying that Christianity doesn't work because Christians sin is a bit like going up to someone who has just started cleaning their house from top to bottom and claiming that what they are doing isn't working because most of the house is still a mess.

Secondly, it assumes that everyone who calls himself a Christian is actually a Christian. But the Bible is pretty clear that there are an awful lot of impostors out there: 'Not every one that saith unto me, Lord, Lord, shall enter into the kingdom of heaven; but he that doeth the will of my Father which is in heaven' (Matthew 7:21). Could it be that some of the worse things committed by 'Christians' were not committed by Christians at all but by those who wore the badge but never actually subscribed?

Thirdly, of course Christians do bad things—the Bible is full of exhortations to believers to forsake their sins, which is a pretty explicit recognition that they do sin. Take the fourth chapter of Ephesians, which among other things tells Christians to 'put away lying' and to 'speak every man truth with his neighbour'; to 'steal no more'; to 'let no corrupt communication proceed out of your mouth'; and to 'let all bitterness, and wrath, and anger, and clamour, and evil speaking, be put away from you, with all malice'. All of which kind of suggests that the believers in Ephesus included liars, thieves, those with foul mouths and those with evil thoughts.

Fourthly, are Christians really no different from anyone else? Much of the answer to this hinges on whether an unbeliever would even recognize and react positively if they noticed a Christian who was becoming less sinful. If a man stops blaspheming, stops getting drunk, stops ogling women, stops swearing, stops coveting, stops gossiping and suchlike, do unbelievers say, 'Wow! That man truly has the Holy Spirit in him, and I can see the promised cleansing from sins being fulfilled in front of my very eyes!' If they do, they will probably end up becoming Christians themselves. But the ones that don't will often end up mocking the Christian, marking him down as a 'saddo' who just doesn't know how to enjoy himself. And so the whole cleansing process is rather lost on such a person.

And one final point. If, as an unbeliever, you look at the Christian and say you see no fulfilment of the promised cleansing because he commits sin, exactly how do you know that he commits sin? Say a pastor commits adultery or steals, on what basis do you condemn him for it? Aren't you using the very law that the Christian is claiming to keep, which just happens to be the law of God? And doesn't the use of this law, which you theoretically deny, undermine your whole position?

'Look,' said Alex, picking up on the last point, 'I have no problem with someone "breaking the law of God" but simply with the hypocrisy of someone who holds to this law, condemns others for breaking it and then goes and breaks it themselves all the same.'

It seems to me that hypocrisy is really the unbeliever's way of getting his own back on the Christian. The Christian has a law—the law of God—that condemns the unbeliever. Although the unbeliever wants to condemn the Christian, he knows he can't appeal to a transcendent law, as such a law could only be given by the God he claims is non-existent. So instead, when Christians break the law of God—which, of course, they do from time to time—the cry goes up from the unbelievers: 'You hypocrites!' Now there are several things that can be said about this.

The first is that in one sense, the unbeliever does have some right to level this accusation at the Christian. Jesus said that his people would be known by their fruits. This does not mean that they would be sinless beings, but it does mean that there must be some conformity to the standard of behaviour and ethics exhibited by Christ himself. If this cannot be found in a person, then they may well be guilty of the charge of being a hypocrite—not because they are a 'sinning Christian' but because they are a 'counterfeit Christian'.

Secondly, it does not follow that a Christian committing a sin is necessarily a hypocrite. It is not hypocrisy to either commit an act that you claim is wrong or to claim that an act you have committed is wrong. Hypocrisy is condemning an act when you are either still committing it yourself or are unrepentant that you have done so in the past. So the acid test is not whether a Christian sins, but this: Does the Christian continue as if nothing was wrong, or is he broken in heart over it? The former is a hypocrite; the latter is a penitent.

Thirdly, to point the finger at Christians as hypocrites when they break the law of God is nothing less than to set up hypocrisy as the highest law of all. It's almost as if the unbeliever is saying that if the Christian who commits adultery had only been an atheist, his adultery would be acceptable because he never claimed it to be wrong.

Fourthly, the unbeliever may well point to the Christian who sins and accuse him of hypocrisy, but is it possible for unbelievers to fall into the pit of hypocrisy as well? Well, of course it is, and it happens just about every time we pass moral judgement on another, for we have undoubtedly committed the very same thing ourselves, whether in our actions, our words or even our thoughts. Which is why Paul warns us that the hypocrisy trap is common to all men: 'Therefore thou art inexcusable, O man, whosoever thou art that judgest: for wherein thou judgest another, thou condemnest thyself; for thou that judgest doest the same things' (Romans 2:1). How do we—both believers and unbelievers—escape from the hypocrisy trap? There is only one way out, and that way is called repentance.

'Do you remember what it was we were discussing before we got a little sidetracked?' I asked when I had finished these points.

'You were going to tell me of all those biblical promises that can apparently be verified by both believers and unbelievers,' replied Alex.

'Ah, that's right,' I replied. 'Well, we certainly don't have time to discuss them all, but some that spring readily to mind are the promises given in the twenty-eighth chapter of Deuteronomy. In that chapter, Moses tells the Israelites of the blessings which will come upon them if they obey God's commandments. These include family blessings ("blessed shall be the fruit of thy body"), economic blessings ("blessed shall be thy basket and thy store") and blessings of peace within their borders ("blessed shalt thou be in the city, and blessed shalt thou be in the field").

'Conversely, if they rejected God's commandments, they would no longer find blessings but curses coming upon them. Their families would disintegrate ("cursed shall be the fruit of thy body"), their prosperity would diminish ("cursed shall be thy basket and thy store"), their peace would be taken from them ("cursed shalt thou be in the city, and cursed shalt thou be in the field") and they would suffer from anxiety, depression and various other mental conditions ("the LORD shall smite thee with madness, and blindness, and astonishment of heart"). Now, which have been the most economically blessed, prosperous, peaceful and free nations? Any guesses?'

Alex didn't answer but simply encouraged me to continue.

'Has it been those that have followed atheistic communism, like the USSR and North Korea? Has it been those that have followed Islam, like Iran and Afghanistan? Or has it been those that have followed biblical Christianity, like the UK, much of northern Europe and North America? And what do we see when those same "Reformation" countries fall like dominoes into secular humanism? Family breakdown, diminished prosperity, high crime and a massive increase in depression and other mental illnesses.

'Or we might take a look at the related issue of freedom. In the book of Proverbs, there are many verses that address this. For example, "For the transgression of the land many are the princes thereof" (Proverbs 28:2— when the Bible uses the word "princes", it doesn't just refer to the monarch's son but to the rulers of a nation). Now, as someone living in a Western nation, it can't have escaped your attention that over the past few years we have had more government, more bureaucrats, more officialdom, more red tape, more political correctness, more interference and more infringements on freedoms than you and I have ever known in our lives. Know what I'm talking about?'

'Yes,' said Alex. 'I have a fair idea.'

'Good,' I continued. 'But did you ever stop to wonder why? Well, you may not have ever considered it before, but is it just coincidence that these things have come about at precisely the same time that the Western nations have abandoned Christianity and the Ten Commandments? Or could it be that after deserting the laws of God, we now find ourselves in a place—and even many unbelievers will admit this—where we are generally less loyal, less trustworthy, less polite, less hardworking and less honest than we used to be, and governments are using this as an excuse to increase their powers to an extent that a moral people would neither need nor tolerate? Could it be that we're seeing the proverb coming true before our very eyes?

'Or perhaps you might want to verify the promises of Christianity by comparing them with the alternatives. Let's take the issue of sexual ethics. Consider the following: imagine two societies, one that strongly advocates faithful, lifelong, heterosexual marriage and disapproves of all other forms of sexual conduct, and the other that strongly advocates promiscuity as a way of life, replete with condom advertisements on television, "sex education" to schoolchildren, morning-after pills and abortion on demand. Now answer me truthfully, Alex: Which one will have the highest rate of sexually transmitted infections? Is this not what you call a "no-brainer"? I put it to you that as the "Thou shalt not commit adultery" society disappears somewhere in the rear-view mirror and the STI rates rise at exactly the same time, someone somewhere maybe ought to twig that the two things are connected and that when God said we would be cursed if we don't keep his laws, he really meant it.'

Not for the first time on that train, Alex proved that he was no dimwit. He said that it was fine for me to bleat on about things like freedom, but maybe I would care to explain to him all those 'freedoms' given to black slaves by Christians in 'enlightened Christian times'. I couldn't resist pointing out that the man most credited with bringing about the end of black slavery—William Wilberforce—did so because he believed it to be utterly incompatible with Christianity.

This brought on a not unexpected response from Alex, who brought up the oft-repeated claim of the unbeliever that the Bible actually sanctions slavery. Well, no! What it sanctions is the keeping of those who sold themselves into servitude and those who had committed certain crimes. But as for the brand of forced slavery imposed on free Africans in the seventeenth and eighteenth centuries, here is what it actually says: 'And he that stealeth a man, and selleth him, or if he be found in his hand, he shall surely be put to death' (Exodus 21:16). That's the Old Testament view, which seems to be pretty clear, wouldn't you say? And in the New Testament, Paul places 'menstealers' on an infamous list of wicked acts that will be judged by God (1 Timothy 1:10). Not much room for doubt there either.

'But of course the Christian nations were not perfect, Alex,' I said. 'Yes, there was slavery based on race practised within Christian nations, and I'm sure that you could bring up many other things that are a blot on our history and a reproach to Christ. But none of this proves that Christianity has failed to fulfil its promises. As I said earlier, so much of the Bible is given over to the admonishing of God's people for this very type of thing—their oppression of others, their neglect of the poor and needy, their refusal to do good to others when they could have and should have.

'Look at the first chapter of Isaiah. It is one long denunciation of God's people for their iniquitous state and a passionate plea for them to turn from their evil ways: "Wash you, make you clean; put away the evil of your doings from before mine eyes; cease to do evil; learn to do well; seek judgment, relieve the oppressed, judge the fatherless, plead for the widow" (Isaiah 1:16–17). The point is that their wickedness is exactly opposite to the commands of the God they claimed as their God. So they needed to turn from these ways or be destroyed.

'But could they do it by themselves? No, for they then needed God to work in their hearts to bring about this change: "Come now, and let us reason together, saith the LORD: though your sins be as scarlet, they shall be as white as snow; though they be red like crimson, they shall be as wool … and I will turn my hand upon thee, and purely purge away thy dross, and take away all thy tin" (Isaiah 1:18, 25).

'Which brings me on to what is the acid test of whether Christianity fulfils its promises or not: don't judge it on whether the world is a war-free zone, nor whether the majority of people love one another selflessly, nor whether Christians lapse into sin. But judge it by what happens when nations and individuals who are steeped in evil and destructive, selfish hedonism truly turn to Jesus Christ and make him their Saviour and Lord. The results are

100 per cent verifiable by both you and me, if we choose to see it. Christianity promises to change the lives of whoever will receive it, and that's precisely what it does. Through the gospel, thieves, gamblers, drug addicts, wife-beaters, drunkards, adulterers, homosexuals, fornicators, manic depressives, liars, abortionists, slave-traders and a whole lot more besides have been utterly changed in a permanent and wonderful way that unbelief has never yet managed to do in changing one single man for the better. And through that gospel you too, Alex, could be utterly changed. But as I say, it only works if you accept it first.'

'Why should I want to change my life? I'm happy with it, and I'm happy the way I am. You haven't said anything today that convinces me that what you believe is the truth, and you haven't said anything today that would induce me to believe it. So why should I? Give me one good reason why I should believe what you believe.'

Objection 10: Give me one good reason why I should believe what you believe

The train was now slowing down as it neared the penultimate stop before my hometown, which meant that we had maybe ten minutes or so to fit in any remaining bits of Life, the Universe and Everything that we had missed. I reckoned this might be a tall order, so I decided to ask Alex if he would be happy to exchange phone numbers, just in case either of us wanted to meet up and talk some more. He told me that he had just that moment been thinking the same thing, and so I pulled my bag down from the overhead luggage rack and took out a pen and a piece of paper to write down his number, while he entered mine into his mobile. I then put my books into my bag and placed it on the seat next to me so that I was all ready to get off at the next station.

Then I turned to Alex's latest objection.

'So you want me to give you one good reason why you should believe what I believe?' I said. 'In a word, "you". I mean that you—Alex—are crucial to all this discussion. We have gone the rounds in what you might describe as a philosophic manner. But ultimately, this is no intellectual thesis we are discussing. This is no philosophical tittle-tattle. It's about you, Alex: you the man, you the bearer of God's image, you the living soul, you the beloved husband and father, you the sinner in need of pardon.

'Now don't misunderstand me. I'm not using the word "you" in a humanistic sense to give you an exalted and egotistical view of yourself. And I'm not saying that you should believe what I want you to believe just in order to make yourself feel better. But I am saying that outside the Christian gospel, you have no satisfactory answers to Life, the Universe and Everything. Your position relies on chance or luck to explain Life and the Universe, but then this leads to some insurmountable problems when it comes to explaining the Everything bit. You are unable to define good and evil starting from luck. You cannot show me how morality came from chance. You are incapable of clarifying what truth, beginning with a silent universe, is. You cannot find a purpose for your life if that life ends with obliteration. And because of this you have no hope.'

He protested against this and tried to raise another objection, but with less than ten minutes left, I decided that by now I was pretty tired of objections and that it was about time Alex justified his position to me for once.

'Okay, Alex,' I said, 'I've done my best to answer all the questions and objections you've thrown at me since we began, but I think it's about time you answered a question or two. So let me throw this one back at you: give me one good reason why I should believe what you believe. No, actually I'm not going to let you off the hook that easily. Give me two reasons: one, why I as a person should believe what you believe; and another, why the world should believe what you believe.'

Alex fudged the question by replying, if not particularly eloquently, 'I don't really care if you believe it or not.'

'Okay, chum,' I thought. 'If that's the way you want to play it, then fine. But with you having subjected me to the "unbeliever's inquisition" for over an hour and a half, insisting that I answer every question and objection thrown at me otherwise it would be taken as a sign that my belief is flawed, I'm sure not letting you off the hook that easily.'

'Fine,' I said. 'You don't have to care if I do believe it or not. But I think that having grilled me since we left Waterloo, you at least owe me some explanation of your own position. So let me rephrase my question: You don't have to tell me why I should believe what you believe, but can you tell me why you believe what you believe?'

Alex responded by giving me what amounted to a chart rundown of perhaps the five most hackneyed objections to Christianity in use today:

5. I'm happy the way I am.
4. Religion is just brainwashing.

Chapter 10

3. I don't need a crutch.
2. Evolution is a fact.
1. There is no God.

You will notice two things about this list: firstly, most of the things on it were things we'd covered during the journey, and with a few minutes left there didn't seem much point in going over any of them again. But the other thing you may have noticed about them is that none of them are what you might call good, positive, hopeful reasons for embracing atheistic, humanistic, evolutionary materialism. So rather than retracing our steps through things already covered, I decided that it would be good to spend the last few minutes talking about hope.

'Of course it gives me hope,' he replied to my asking him if his belief gave him and humanity any hope. 'I have hope for me and my family that our lives will improve, and I see much progress and hope for humanity in general in the world today.'

So the world and I are all heading for annihilation, but I'm really hopeful about the future! One of the best illustrations of the absurdity of this was actually written by a humanist, H. J. Blackham, who said:

On humanist assumptions, life leads to nothing; and every pretense that it does not is a deceit. If there is a bridge over a gorge which spans only half the distance and ends in mid-air, and if the bridge is crowded with human beings pressing on, one after another they fall into the abyss. The bridge leads nowhere and those who are pressing forward to cross it are going nowhere. It does not matter where they think they are going, what preparations for the journey they may have made, how much they may be enjoying it all. The objection merely points out objectively that such a situation is a model of futility.[1]

Where Blackham's illustration falls short of the likes of Alex's position is that no one seems to be aware that the bridge reaches only halfway across the gorge until they find themselves falling over the edge. But in Alex's case, his whole position rests on the belief that he and the world know they are going to fall over the edge, and yet bizarrely he can still talk about hope for the future.

For the last time on the train that day, I borrowed Alex's mobile to find a quote, this time by the late Douglas Adams, author of *The Hitchhiker's Guide to the Galaxy* and an avowed atheist:

I was extremely doubtful about the idea of God, but I just didn't know enough about anything to have a good working model of any other explanation for, well, life, the universe, and everything to put in its place. It [evolution] was a concept of such stunning simplicity, but it gave rise, naturally, to all of the infinite and baffling complexity of life. The awe it inspired in me made the awe that people talk about in respect of religious experience seem, frankly, silly beside it. I'd take the awe of understanding over the awe of ignorance any day.[2]

As an aside, it seems pretty apparent from the first sentence in this quote that he had already decided that he didn't want to believe in God before he actually found his 'reason' not to, don't you think? He was obviously looking for a way to rid himself of God once and for all, and over time he apparently discovered his get-out clause—evolution— clearly rejoicing at the effect this revelation had on him.

'You know,' I said to Alex after reading the quote to him, 'I agree with him about understanding and ignorance. But sadly, the whole quote shows that he was perfectly ignorant of that which he claimed as understanding.'

'And why is that?' said Alex.

'Well, before I make my point, please understand that I am not commenting on the truth or falsehood of his belief. Let me repeat that, just in case you misunderstand me: I am not commenting on the truth or falsehood of his belief. That's another subject entirely, and we've covered some of it today anyway. What I'm discussing here is purely the issue of hope. Somehow, Douglas Adams seemed to think that making his "discovery" that there is no God was a marvellous thing and something to be celebrated. But I wonder if, in the euphoria of casting off God, he ever really stopped to reason with himself on this one. Had he done so, I reckon his euphoria would have turned to depression pretty quickly.'

Again Alex questioned my assertion, so I put it like this: let's just say that Douglas Adams had once accepted the Christian God. What would that have meant to him? Here are seven things:

1. He would have known that the universe was made by God and so is not just a purposeless machine.
2. He would have known that he was made in the image of God and so was a creature with a purpose.
3. He would have known that the God who made him was deeply interested in him.
4. He would have known that although he was alienated from this God because he had violated his laws, God was prepared to show abundant mercy to him.
5. He would have known that this God listened to him in his joys and his heartaches.
6. He would have known that when troubles and afflictions came upon him, there was a personal being behind the universe who cared and would help him.
7. He would have known that this God had prepared a place for him in an everlasting abode where his purpose would be fulfilled and he would be always happy.

Now imagine that he goes off this idea and makes his 'discovery' about evolution. What should this have meant to him? Here are seven conclusions he would have come to if he had been thinking straight:

1. He would have realized that the universe was nothing but a gigantic, purposeless machine.
2. He would have realized that as a creature made in the image of dust, he was nothing but a purposeless cog in the purposeless machine.
3. He would have realized that the universe couldn't care less about him, what he did or didn't do, whether he was happy or sad, whether he was 'moral' or 'immoral', whether he lived or died.

4. He would have realized that the alienation and the loneliness he sometimes felt from the universe, from other people and even from himself was 100 per cent real but with no remedy.

5. He would have realized that the universe was completely cold and silent to any of his thoughts and desires.

6. He would have realized that when troubles and afflictions came upon him, the universe couldn't care less about him.

7. He would have realized that he would be annihilated in a few more years or days or hours or minutes, and then he would be nothing—nothing, nothing, nothing.

When I finished, Alex did exactly what I had asked him not to do—make some comment about it proving that my belief is a crutch and that I'm just not able to cope with the truth.

'I told you not to do that, Alex,' I said, tutting and shaking my head as if admonishing a naughty schoolboy. 'I said that I wasn't commenting on whether it is true or not but rather what your reaction should be if it is true. Assume that the Bible is true. What reaction ought you to have? Nothing but joy! The universe is not silent. There is a loving God out there. You have purpose. Life is not meaningless. You can have forgiveness for your sins, and you can have everlasting life. Now assume that evolutionary materialism is true. What reaction ought you to have? Joy? Of course—we're all just highly evolved bits of dust living an often painful existence on an often wicked planet; we try to find a purpose, but it's all to no avail because there isn't one, and we're heading for obliteration. Oh joy! Oh joy! Oh joy!'

'Like I say, you just can't accept it,' said Alex, again missing the point I was making.

'No, Alex,' I replied. 'We are not talking about whether it is true or not. We've done all that for today. We are talking about what it means if it is true. Let me put it like this: if your position is true, I'll accept it. Only please don't expect me to get all misty-eyed, lip-quivery and lump-in-the-throatish about it, because if it is true, it goes down as the most awful, depressing, sad, miserable, horrible truth I could imagine. What an answer to Life, the Universe and Everything is this!

'But Douglas Adams seemed to think that finding out he was a pointless cog in the machine destined for extermination in a cold, silent, pointless universe was a jolly happy discovery. I suspect that his real jubilation lay not in discovering that he was a pointless piece of dying dust—I doubt whether he ever even considered what this really meant—but in finding a so-called "intellectual" reason for killing off God in his conscience. But if he'd actually understood this, the joke answer he gave to the question of Life, the Universe and Everything in *The Hitchhiker's Guide to the Galaxy* wouldn't have been forty-two; it would have been zero—ABSOLUTE NOTHING.

'Now how you can get any joy or hope out of this is bizarre beyond words. Just like that book you have there,' I said, pointing to his copy of *The God Delusion*. 'What's it called? *The Odd Delusion*, is it? It sure is an odd delusion that despises the idea of a God offering us salvation and eternal happiness but falls head over heels in love with the idea of total annihilation. I think this is what is meant when Christ says in the book of Proverbs that "all they that hate me love death" (Proverbs 8:36).'

He was silent for a few moments while he chewed this over. I could tell that he wanted to make the point again about me not being able to accept the truth but thought the better of bringing it up for a third time, perhaps fearing that I might just sit there and growl at him. Instead he went down the 'hope for humanity' road, mentioning all the kinds of things that apparently show just how much progress humanity is making.

'Sorry, Alex, but there is no more point in trying to find hope for humanity within your purely materialistic worldview than there is in finding hope for the individual. By its very nature, your worldview cannot offer any hope, because one of its fundamental pillars is that we are all to be obliterated back to the dust. The fact that there are seven billion blobs of dust destined for obliteration doesn't make the slightest difference. It just means that seven billion such entities will fall into the abyss when they try to cross the gorge. The answer to Life, the Universe and Everything—according to your worldview—is still zero. Seven billion times zero, but still zero.

'So when you hear all this stuff about saving the planet and all that, wake up and smell the coffee! Quite apart from the issue of whether today's so-called threats are actually threats at all and quite apart from the issue of whether we could do anything about them if they were—which are both discussions for another day—it doesn't matter! Within your worldview, there is no good reason why I should care a fig whether the earth dies a heat death or freezes over or is blown to smithereens. Would it matter one way or the other? Not really. Would it make me a good, altruistic person if I did care about it? Would it make me a bad, uncharitable sort if I didn't care about it? Does any of it matter? Not a bit of it. If annihilation is the destiny of all of us and the universe, who cares whether it comes today, tomorrow or at some distant point in the future?

'All this has come about because in rejecting the only real Saviour of men—Jesus Christ, the eternal Son of God—men have a need to project themselves as saviours. So they invent their spurious threats—global cooling yesterday, global warming today, maybe global tepidness tomorrow—purely in order that they can pose as saviours of mankind. But the whole thing is a giant con trick. Even if their theories were correct, and even if they were able to control the temperatures on planet Earth, how many people would they have saved? None whatsoever! We will still all die, humanity will one day die and that will be that.'

Alex gave no answer! He could give no answer because there is no answer to this within his worldview. This is journey's end for materialistic, atheistic humanism. Maybe you believe it to be the truth, but don't you try to glean a single grain of hope from it. It can give you none. It ends in nothing but death—death for you, death for me, death for Alex, death for everyone. Any hope you take from it is merely an illusion—worse than that, a delusion.

If you are an unbeliever truly seeking answers to Life, the Universe and Everything, and you truly understand this point, you will despair. But as I told Alex on the train that day, there is no need to despair. For there are answers and there is hope. Christianity gives the answers to the questions of Life, the Universe and Everything that we desperately need—answers that explain the origins of life without invoking 'some luck to get it started'; answers that tell us who we really are without making monkeys out of us; answers that tell us of an infinite and personal being behind the universe who does not leave us to rot in a lost and lonely world; answers that establish right from wrong and truth from falsehood rather than leaving us to drown in a sea of relativism; answers that give us a genuine and eternal purpose rather than leaving us with the impossible task of finding a purpose within a world destined for obliteration; answers that give us both order and freedom in society rather than the twin evils of anarchy and despotism that humanism bequeaths; and answers that give us hope of forgiveness for our wrongdoing and joyous life everlasting, whereas unbelief only offers us the morbid prospect of oblivion.

Where are the answers? They are found in the Bible, which has withstood all attempts of tyrants, anarchists, sceptics, popes and scientists to expunge it. Where is the hope? The hope is found in this: 'In Christ God was reconciling the world to himself, not counting their trespasses against them, and entrusting to us the message of reconciliation … For our sake he made him to be sin who knew no sin, so that in him we might become the righteousness of God' (2 Corinthians 5:19, 21).

'Go read it, Alex,' I said. 'Go get answers. Go find hope.'

Notes

1 Quoted in *A Christian View of the West* in *The Complete Works of Francis Schaeffer*, vol. 5 (Carlisle: Paternoster, 1998), p. 355.
2 Quoted in Richard Dawkins, *The God Delusion* (London: Black Swan, 2007), pp. 141–142.

Journey's end

By now the train was pulling into my hometown station. Our conversation finished, I thanked Alex for talking to me and said that I was sorry we didn't get to cover all of Life, the Universe and Everything, but that perhaps one day we would meet up again and get to talk some more. He said he would certainly like to do that as he had what he called 'one or two questions of a more practical nature to put to me'. I replied that I would maybe give him a call in a couple of weeks and we could arrange something. Then after I had put my jumper and coat on and picked up my bag, I shook his hand and wished him God's blessing, and then I was off.

As I stepped off the train and began the short walk to my house, I thought a great deal about the conversation I'd had. As always, a whole load of things that I should have said came into my mind, plus a whole load of things I probably shouldn't have said and then a whole load of things that I should have said in a better way.

But my biggest regret was that I felt that I should have shown him more love. It's so often the case that when one gets into such a conversation with a hardened unbeliever, the conversation moves into intellectual territory. Not that this is wrong. True Christianity always affects the head before it affects the heart. And in any case, if someone dismissively asks 'What is truth?' you can't just reply with 'For God so loved the world, that he gave his only begotten Son, that whosoever believeth in him should not perish, but have everlasting life' (John 3:16). They will just laugh at you. No, you've got to address them where they're at, before they are even close to listening to John 3:16. But it's often the way that in the midst of such a discussion, we can lose sight of the fact that this is a person in front of us—a human being made in the image of God, with emotions, hopes, desires and needs, and we ought to love them as such.

I reflected too that Alex and his like occupy two positions. On the one hand, they are so far from the kingdom of heaven as to seem utterly

Chapter 10

unreachable. But on the other hand, the kingdom of heaven is so accessible to everyone with a pulse that it is as close as the distance Alex and I had sat from one another. All it takes is a humbling of the heart, repentance of sins and trust in Jesus Christ, and that vast chasm of separation is bridged in an instant.

It is both frustrating and thrilling: frustrating that all the talking in the world cannot change a heart one bit—only God can do this—but thrilling because it is often through such conversations that God does change hearts. I knew that I had some serious praying to do that night for Alex.

I wondered too what he would be thinking about on his way home. Would he be quietly sniggering to himself? Or would he be thinking seriously upon some of the things we had discussed? And I wondered what he would tell his wife when he got in. Would he talk dismissively about meeting some 'Jesus freak' or 'God botherer' on the train, or would he give a fair account of our discussion and have a proper conversation with her about these great issues?

As I walked up the hill to my home, I suddenly realized how utterly drained I was. During such conversations, the adrenalin flows abundantly, but when it comes to the end, a strange sensation of emotional exhaustion often comes over. So I was glad when I came to my front door and saw my dear wife and children looking out the window, waiting for me with outstretched arms and beaming smiles. As they bustled to open the door, I thanked God for the conversation I had had; I thanked him for preserving me; and I thanked him for my beautiful family within. And with that, the door closed and I reached my journey's end. I was home.